Software Life Cycle Management Standards

Real-world Scenarios and Solutions for Savings

Software Life Cycle Management Standards

Real-world Scenarios and Solutions for Savings

DAVID WRIGHT

IT Governance Publishing

IT Governance Publishing
IT Governance Limited
Unit 3, Clive Court
Bartholomew's Walk
Cambridgeshire Business Park
Ely
Cambridgeshire
CB7 4EH
United Kingdom

www.itgovernance.co.uk

First published in the United Kingdom in 2011
by IT Governance Publishing.

ISBN 978-1-84928-204-8

FOREWORD

David Wright has addressed an important topic with this book, providing a valuable resource for people involved in architecting and implementing the technologies of software management. David has written the book from the perspective of a real-world practitioner, and it should help other real-world practitioners understand and exploit the technology. Don't read it for theory; read it for practical ideas and guidance.

The technology is based on the ISO/IEC 19770-2:2009 software identification tag (SWID). This technology is starting to be adopted by many different software vendors and tool providers, but at the time of writing is still in the process of adoption. This book should help in that adoption, written by someone who has extensive practical experience with one of the first software vendors to adopt SWID tagging.

The question may be asked as to why this technology is needed. The purpose of the SWID is to optimise the identification and management of software. This seems so simple and basic that it is almost impossible to believe that it is needed. Is it not true that software is already being identified by a plethora of software discovery tools? And is software not already being managed? Why do we need a new technology to achieve this?

The question may be answered in two different ways. The first is to cite the details of the problems which exist in current, inconsistent and inaccurate approaches to software identification. These are well documented in many places, with TagVault.org being one of the best sources of such information. However, many people do not want to believe this, or that the implications are significant enough to worry about. They essentially have a policy of benign neglect. This leads us to the second way of answering the question. Many, if not most, CTOs/CIOs will think they are sufficiently in control of their software assets to get by. And most SAM or ITAM managers will communicate to senior management that they are in control because their jobs depend on it and they have a commercial SAM tool which they trust to do competent discovery and management for them. Yet there is a credibility gap here. How is it that software publishers or their agents can conduct audit after audit of organisations which consider themselves in control and repeatedly come up with multimillion-dollar compliance findings – for individual publishers? Ask any one of the CTOs/CIOs which have been burnt by these findings whether they have the information they need to ensure licensing compliance and you will almost certainly be told 'no'. Inaccurate software identification is a major part of the problem.

Security is another issue which is typically overlooked when considering software identification, in part because SAM and security live in different 'silos'. Yet work by US government agencies to identify the most important controls to prevent known compromises – not just theoretical ones – has identified that the top four controls are all effectively SAM and ITAM controls. (*See www.sans.org/critical-security-controls*.) Knowing what you have on your network is basic SAM and is basic security. The SWID tag is likely to become a major part of much of the future IT security infrastructure. This book gives some information on these developments and more recent information should be available on TagVault.org.

Let me end this foreword with an analogy which may speak to the older IT generation and may teach the younger IT generation something as well. I started my career in consultancy in the 1970s by spending quite some time with material requirement planning (MRP). I see strong parallels between the development of that area with the development of SAM today. Inventory management was a lose–lose area in which to work – you either did not have stock when you needed it or you had too much, and nobody thanked you when you got it right. MRP improved that dramatically, but it was only the start. Then came kanban, or just-in-time, external supplier integration and then full supply chain integration. It eventually became the innocuously named area of logistics, which seldom gets the limelight but which makes or breaks most companies dealing in physical products. The analogy is this: the advent of tagging for software management is equivalent to the advent of MRP for physical goods management. There is still a long way we can go, but it is a quantum leap forward from the old world of inventory control using reorder points. Software asset control without tagging is like living in the dark ages or worse – software identification using today's methods has been called identification through archaeology. This book can help you learn about the future and make it happen.

David Bicket

David Bicket is Convener of the working group responsible for international SAM standards (ISO/IEC JTC1 SC7 WG21). He project-managed and wrote a significant part of the *ITIL SAM Guide* (2003), and had major responsibility for the development of ISO/IEC 19770-1:2006 software asset management processes. He may be contacted via the WG21 website (*www.19770.org*).

PREFACE

I have to say that as a child, I did not lay awake at night dreaming of a career in Software Life Cycle Management or International Standards. Then as I reached my youth, like many of my peers in the late 60s and early 70s, I saw a future for myself as a musician and leader of the rock band I toured with while a student at university in England. Ultimately, reality took hold and after many attempts to decide what I wanted to be when I grew up, not to mention a variety of geographic locations (some of which I will be happy never to visit again), I landed in Silicon Valley, California, put down my roots in nearby Santa Cruz, just south of 'The Valley' then built a career in software engineering and IT systems.

I still love music, which is playing constantly in my office, my car, in my headset while running on the beach and occasionally in my head when dreaming. But in the meantime, I must admit that I have found my intellectual niche, wondering about and attempting to analyse and model the real-world problems in high-tech commerce.

Perhaps not as glamorous as my youthful images of fame and fortune, the constant changes and evolution that come about as a result of the creative minds by whom I am surrounded in one of the most dynamic environments in the world today is, for me, probably more stimulating.

In fact, events transpired so quickly during the writing that I found passages written early in the process became outdated and needed revising by the end of the project.

So you, the reader, should probably understand several criteria as you digest the contents herein:

- By the time my words here have been edited, compiled, formatted and reproduced, there will have been further progress and although I will attempt frequent revisions, I and my (already!) long-suffering publisher, ITGP, may not be able to keep pace with the rate of change. There is a website you can go to – *www.lifecyclestandards.com* – where I will try and keep you updated on changes, although the book revisions will occur only with ITGP's help.
- I don't have all of the answers, even should evolution stand still. In fact, I hope the morning never arrives when I wake up with all the answers and no questions. I welcome all comments and inputs and have supplied here an e-mail address with which to provide your feedback – *info@authordavidwright.com*. Your input will be gratefully accepted and with your permission could well be included in future revisions of this book. I have a wife and four children who have shredded my ego to pieces, so do not be afraid to speak your mind.
- Although I am interested in ensuring that this book is easy to read and not reserved for late-night reading by insomniacs, I have made every attempt to ensure that what is presented here is accurate and of real-world use. While not an academic tome, I hope you will find the facts described to be a useful reference.
- The calculations on savings and benefits to the end-user are based on what I think are the currently accepted costs of today's manual processes compared with the pricing model and tag density estimates that emanate from my work at VeriTag. There is, I am sure, room for error in

my assumptions and any feedback will be gratefully received for inclusion in any revisions.

- The book is aimed at both managers and technicians. As a result, there are some chapters (6, 7 and 8) which dig deeply into specifics of the standards. However, even if this is too detailed for you, don't let this stop you from exploring the later chapters as a manager. These later sections are where I try to pinpoint areas of process and financial savings.

Lastly, what you are about to read will give you, I hope, an overview of the software life cycle and its management, as well as very precise specifics as to how the ISO/IEC 19770 standards are applied and, in my opinion, help to simplify as well as reduce costs in a difficult field of endeavour.

ABOUT THE AUTHOR

I was born in Luton, UK, the eldest son of, yes, a Vauxhall Motors plant worker who was married to a hatter's daughter. When I was five years old, my father decided to strike out for a better life and, accompanied by my supportive mother and baby brother, took us to the Sudan to seek a fortune in the British Empire. Rule Britannia!

Returning after several years to the UK, with fortune in hand, my mother and father invested their hard-earned savings into starting a new business, which still exists today under the direction of my 'baby' brother.

Later on, while still studying at university, I was given the chance to be involved in the design of an early remote-sensing system, used for astronomical applications, at the University of British Columbia. Repeated trips, before and after graduation, to Vancouver BC convinced me that North America, especially the West Coast, was where I wanted to be. I once again became the expatriate Englishman.

After several years of working in Canada and Europe, I was given the chance to come to California on a 90-day project. That was in June 1981. I still have not left California, although I did complete that project on time!

Since that time I have continued working on many projects in Silicon Valley, some allowing me to travel elsewhere in the world. This career has allowed me to remain based here in the old-fashioned beach community of Santa Cruz where I make my home with my beautiful Californian wife and family.

About the Author

I love to spend time running through the harbour and on to the beach, and even occasionally like to take a route through the Santa Cruz Beach Boardwalk with its old-fashioned rides. There I am reminded of my childhood trips to the seaside as I absorb the excited screams of thrilled riders and drink in the aroma of popcorn, hot dogs, ice cream and sunscreen lotion.

Life could be worse!

ACKNOWLEDGEMENTS

Special thanks must go to my talented and long-suffering wife, Michele (who photographed the background image of the Santa Cruz Beach Boardwalk Ferris Wheel on the cover of this book), and two college-aged sons, DJ and Alex, who have suffered through my long weeks of inadequate attention to their needs. This is not to mention *me* occasionally snapping at *them* when 'disturbed' by their loving attention to me during my moments of intense focus. Sometimes I can be too single-minded. I apologise to you all.

Next, thanks go to my business partner and good friend of 25 years, Hal Shores, who has encouraged me continually through this process to express my views, ideas and observations in a book. He and Michele have almost tied for the number of times of telling me when to stop working and take time on the beach!

The majority of ideas expressed in this book originated with the people listed below. I can only claim to have assembled those ideas into one place, hopefully accurately, and have mixed in the sauce in order to create the final product.

John Richardson and Mairead Kavanagh at Symantec Corporation, both of whom I have had the pleasure of working with on software licensing and service challenges over several years: thank you both for your very explicit contributions to this book, on philosophy, ideas and process design.

Many hours have been spent in conference calls or in face-to-face sessions, engaging frequently in spirited discussions on the topic of ISO/IEC 19770 and associated subjects, with:

- Dave Bicket, ISO/IEC JTC1/SC7/WG21 Convener
- Steve Klos, convener of the ISO/IEC 19770-2 Working Group and now executive director of TagVault.org
- John Tomeny, convener of the ISO/IEC 19770-3 Working Group.

Participating members of those working groups that have assisted me, sometimes without realising perhaps, in expressing or forming the ideas expressed here include: Krzysztof (Chris) Bączkiewicz, standards document editor and XSD 'king', Juan Carlos Colosso, Robin Trebec, Mary Barr, Karen Grunebach, Steve Mullins, Venkatesh Somashekhar, Doc Burnham, Mathieu Baissac and Mika Harviala.

Grateful thanks are due to Antonio Velasco, CEO, Sinersys Technologies, for his helpful review of the manuscript.

I must acknowledge the wonderful publishing team at ITGP, including Publishing Manager, Angela Wilde, and Pat Winfield, a copy-editor with an extraordinary eye for detail plus an ability to uncover then correct my errors, both content and language, without chastising me as did my grammar school English Language teacher, Miss Moss.

Lastly, but not least, a thank you has to go to Cris Wendt, expert and blogger on most of the topics discussed here. Cris graciously gave up time to read everything I have written in an effort to weed out any stupid statements I made. We have spent many hours over coffee or lunch pondering life's challenges, not just those confined to the contents addressed in this book. If I had to pick an intellectual brother, he would be my man.

CONTENTS

INTRODUCTION

The goal of this book

It seems to me that unless I can explain the ultimate goal and associated benefits that might be achieved by all that I describe in this book, there is really very little point in you reading on; so here is a simple statement that encapsulates all that the ideas expressed here aspire to:

Quantifying the value delivered by software/SaaS and removing the 'us versus them' framework between publisher and customer in enterprise software commerce.

I must say that if you don't find this concept appealing and you are standing in a bookshop trying to decide if the book in your hand interests you or not, then close it up right now and put it back on the shelf.

If you have reached this paragraph, then you are either a glutton for punishment or the topic is of interest to you. At least, your interest is at the level that you would like to explore the concepts of software life cycle management, including the component of software asset management (SAM), and how emerging standards can be successfully applied to these practices in order to improve the results derived.

A basic premise for the ideas expressed here is that the software life cycle does not start with the consumer purchasing the licensed or service product. It starts with a gleam in the eye of a product manager and is carried all the way through a cycle that touches everyone involved: publisher, third-party/original equipment manufacturer (OEM)/channel partner and consumer, and spans many phases, often across many years. These standards offer the opportunity to connect and manage co-operatively, between all concerned if so desired, across that entire life cycle; something that thus far has not been achievable.

For those of you that are concerned with managing and maintaining an IT department that is increasingly dependent upon the Cloud and its services, the standards may have answers to some of the problems you either already face or may face in the future.

This book covers two main components of the ISO/IEC 19770 standard: ISO/IEC 19770-2:2009 software component identification (SWID) tagging, and ISO/IEC 19770-3 software entitlement identification (SWEID) tagging. While the latter is not yet accepted by ISO, I hope that by the time this publication is available, the draft of the standard will be accepted and under consideration for publication within the next few months. Perhaps you can use the mechanisms for usage and a rough preview of the structures illustrated here in anticipation of the full standard being available.

Also worth noting, in my opinion, are the possibilities for exploitation of the standards prior to their complete acceptance and use by all software publishers. There are notable leaders on the publishing side (the latest list can be found at *www.tagvault.org*) as well as significant end-user promotion of the standard by more forward-thinking institutions such as the US Government and its various departments.

There are gains and savings available for an enterprise consumer of software, even in the short term, in implementing ISO/IEC 19770-based technology and processes. There are existing methods to do so, even if your software supplier is not obliging you with adoption of the standards.

On the other side, publishers who sell to the US Government are in danger of being left in the dust by those publishers that have adopted these standards, as some mandates for their use are already place by departments within the US Federal Government.

Please read on and I will attempt to share ideas, some of my own, as well as those of others immersed in the software management field. During our journey I will share opinions, anecdotes and facts, some of which I hope you will find informative as well as entertaining.

CHAPTER 1: SOFTWARE ASSET MANAGEMENT: BOTH SIDES OF THE EQUATION

Overview

A software publisher rarely allows the software itself to be sold. The publisher sells rights, or entitlements, to use via the sale of licences. The risk to both the customer and the publisher is that software deployment and usage is very difficult to measure. Even the term usage is very difficult to define and must be described very specifically as part of the 'right to use' or licence.

Such confusion can give rise to two dominant questions for the IT manager:

1 Am I using more or less than I am entitled to?
2 Am I optimising usage across all my titles such that I am getting business value for my expenditure?

The single rule that governs whether a customer is in compliance with respect to their software asset is that for every deployment there must be an entitlement that allows the deployment.

A simple view of this situation is shown in Figure 1. On one hand, on the left, is the entitlement for use as defined in the licence or software right-to-use agreement. On the other hand, on the right, is the representation of how the software is actually used, that is to say the deployment and usage of features provided as defined in the agreement. This balance is described as reconciliation and ideally should always be in complete balance. When a measurement is made, if the reconciliation matches, i.e. there is a zero reconciliation gap, then the two hands clap. I like to picture this as applause, which of course becomes louder as a greater number of agreements are sold and greater amounts of software are used.

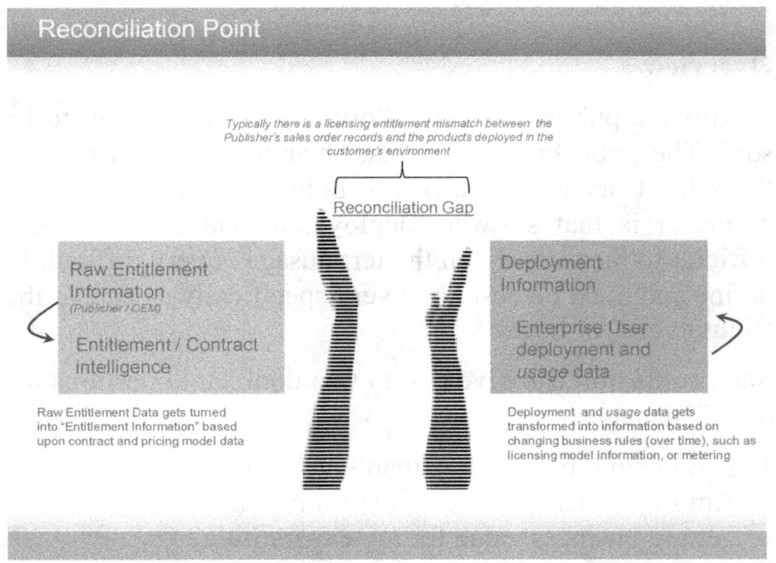
Reconciliation Point
Typically there is a licensing entitlement mismatch between the Publisher's sales order records and the products deployed in the customer's environment
Reconciliation Gap
Raw Entitlement Information
(Publisher / OEM)
Entitlement / Contract intelligence
Deployment Information
Enterprise User deployment and usage data
Raw Entitlement Data gets turned into "Entitlement Information" based upon contract and pricing model data
Deployment and usage data gets transformed into information based on changing business rules (over time), such as licensing model information, or metering

Figure 1: Reconciliation gap

Reconciliation gaps are a problem for both the end-user and the publisher and provide a barrier to a sound relationship between the two sides.

Even if there is a zero compliance gap, this does not necessarily mean the user is deriving value from software expenditure. This is where the concept of use becomes hazy. Just because a software title is installed, it does not necessarily mean it is being used. Further, if a single title is installed in two places, but only used by one user at a time, the user may have purchased twice the true entitlement needed because the publisher licenses only by seat, not by concurrent users.

I could write several chapters here on licensing models, but this book is not designed to address that topic. However, what I do want to discuss here is the ability to measure these different models, using standards-based technology. Both the vendor/publisher and the consumer should be able to engage in software commerce with a clear understanding of expectations and deliverables on both sides, and both should be able to optimise their business for profits in their respective fields without confusion or the practice of black magic.

Compliance: the delicate balance that rules software commerce

Depending upon the 'go to market' scenario through which an entitlement was delivered/granted, at one extreme there may be a unique entitlement(s) for each deployment. At the other extreme, there may be a blanket agreement that allows unlimited deployment. Of course there exists every case in between. There is also the consideration that for most large enterprise customers, deployments of different products may have been granted as a result of multiple agreements, which in turn have probably been made at different times, perhaps even with different channel suppliers for the same product. To complicate matters further, there may be multiple agreements in place concurrently. Thus entitlement management and the understanding of entitlement is a very complex process that can change depending upon the point in time at which the entitlement measurement is taken.

When corresponding deployments are measured in order to match against entitlements, the licence model or business rules for product usage for any given product frequently change from release to release. Therefore, it is important to attempt to identify each deployment uniquely as well as understand the version and release date for each product deployment.

In this situation, the deployment report could look identical for the two different versions of the product since the functional model is the same for each. However, the entitlement purchases may be different for each and therefore have an impact on the compliance assessment.

To further complicate matters, the entitlement for any single deployment may not be valid for another deployment of an identical release as the business rules governing the entitlement for any deployment may be unique.

Figure 2 illustrates the four-layer approach to compliance. As can be seen, in the compliance scenario, simply understanding the deployment and the individual licences acquired is not sufficient to understand whether compliance is in place or not. It is necessary to understand the model for each individual deployment, and the contract terms under which the licence was acquired.

Such confusion can easily present a problem in the relationship between the customer and the vendor. Therefore, once an acquirer (end-user) has received both software and licence, it is desirable for both the supplier and the user that the usage of the software matches the entitlement or licence to use.

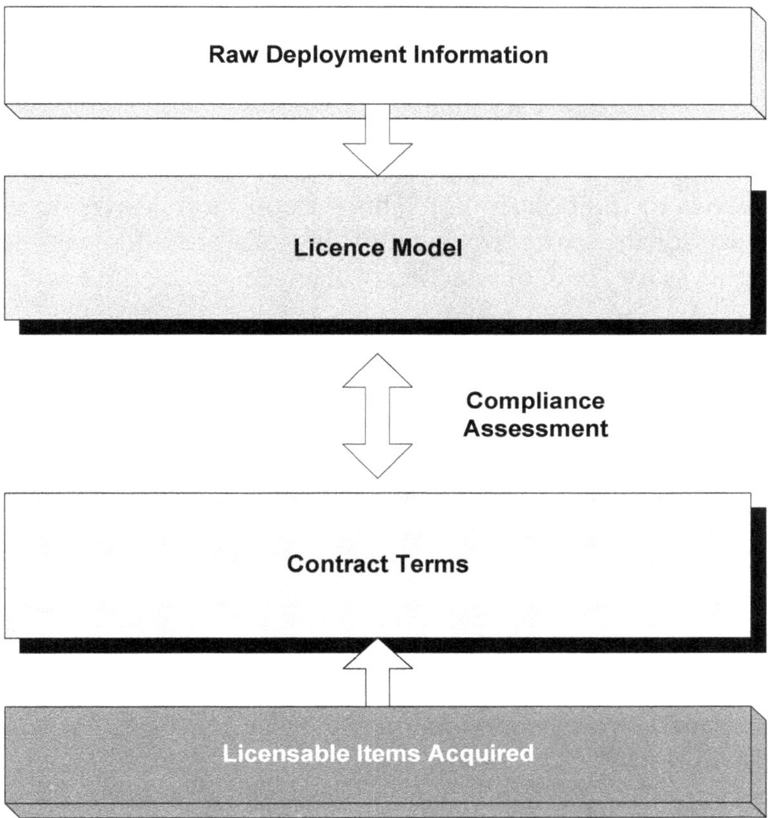

Figure 2: Four-layer approach to compliance

This paradigm is fundamental to the concept of compliance.

The single rule that governs whether a customer is in compliance with respect to their software asset is that for every deployment there must be an entitlement that allows the specific deployment, including the usage of that deployment.

Compliance is a common goal for both supplier and consumer, but for different reasons. The consumer, or end-user, wishes to ensure that they do not purchase more rights to use than needed, and the supplier wishes to ensure that the end-user does not use the supplied software beyond the bounds of the right to use. This situation should remain in place for the entire life cycle of the software usage and its rights to use, both of which may change over the life cycle.

True value: the software consumer's continual quest

I doubt that anyone reading here would bother to rent a car, take it home and then just let it sit in the driveway (unless trying to impress the neighbours with the fact that they have such an exotic machine at their disposal of course!). Value is using our resources in the optimum fashion.

For instance, if I have one car and it can be used 24/7 by multiple people who never need simultaneous access and the terms of car usage allow for such an arrangement, then perhaps I am close to optimising value. However, if one driver wishes to transport eight people at a time, another only needs to transport two, and yet another wishes to carry bales of hay, then there may be further issues of size (meter) and functionality with the single vehicle.

If the vehicle is rented, there may also be further complications added by the entitlement. Perhaps there are restrictions on the load, on the mileage travelled per day or on the hours used.

Software is no different when regarded as a resource. Often, however, it cannot be functionally identified in deployment, usage or entitlement. Not only does the licensing model not support varied types of usage, the measurement of such usage is not possible.

Software as a service

Software as a service (SaaS) is a technology that is emerging as a replacement for licensed software in some places and will no doubt continue to grow and prove more useful as time goes on. We are continually bombarded by concepts of the Cloud by the media these days. The notion that this is new or the next big thing is quite valid; from a practical and architectural point of view, the so-called Cloud has existed for many years.

The current version is an evolution of a concept that did not catch on at the end of the twentieth century: application service providers (ASPs). ASPs were supposed to provide out-of-the-box functionality with minimal requirements for on-site software and software management. Unfortunately, the implementations were based upon traditional software architectures and proved to be as expensive to maintain, if not more so, than in-house applications and the ASP concept failed miserably.

As soon as applications started to be implemented using Internet technologies and architecture, the ability to build multi-tenant applications (such as Salesforce.com) was made easier and there is now an exploding set of offerings in a variety of business applications.

Despite the more managed nature of SaaS, there are still aspects of overall management that have issues that are yet to be solved in a standard cross-platform manner. Some of these issues may be overcome by the appropriate application of ISO/IEC 19770 ID tags in order to ease the pain.

The issues of entitlement management remain very much the same. It is critical to understand and manage entitlements, whether they be for licensed software usage or SaaS usage. Understanding usage against these entitlements is, of course, slightly different for each one. While the measurement of software usage is challenging, as outlined above for licensed software, similar issues are there for SaaS also:

- The entitlement model for the service offered may not be appropriate in order to understand true value.
- Any usage information can only be derived from the service vendor, which may not match the usage perception of the consumer.
- A method to match vendor-generated usage information with a standard form of entitlement information supplied by multiple services does not exist.
- For many years to come, Cloud-based services will need to interoperate with licensed software in a user environment, thus a common usage measurement system with a single source of truth is required.
- There is a need in the service's life cycle management for an understanding of the current state and history of service usage from a feature, meter and version point of view. This information may be required in a consolidated fashion across multiple providers and licensed software applications, so simply using provider information is not adequate.

- Internal Cloud services need to be maintained by a user/consumer with just the same rigour as licensed software.

The software product life cycle

My view of a life cycle was so simple when I only had to consider that of the lowly amoeba! Today, we are bombarded with the concept of life cycles. Everything in my life has a life cycle, according to the guy down at the DIY store. Of course, that guy oversimplifies the issue. If it's broken, the useful life cycle is over and I need to replace it with a new, improved, shinier model. Whatever happened to the tool repair truck that went round sharpening tools and repairing broken ones? But that is a story for another day.

Software is no simpler of course; there are several intersecting life cycles, some depending upon your point of view, provider or consumer perhaps, some depending upon your role.

ISO/IEC 19770-2 SWID tag management and the proposed ISO/IEC 1977-3 SWEID tags allow, to some extent, quantitative measurement of software deployment, software usage and software entitlement. Figure 3 illustrates a software product life cycle and where these tags may be used by both the software publisher and the software consumer for management purposes.

The concept of a software product life cycle is the foundation for all arguments and ideas I present in this book!

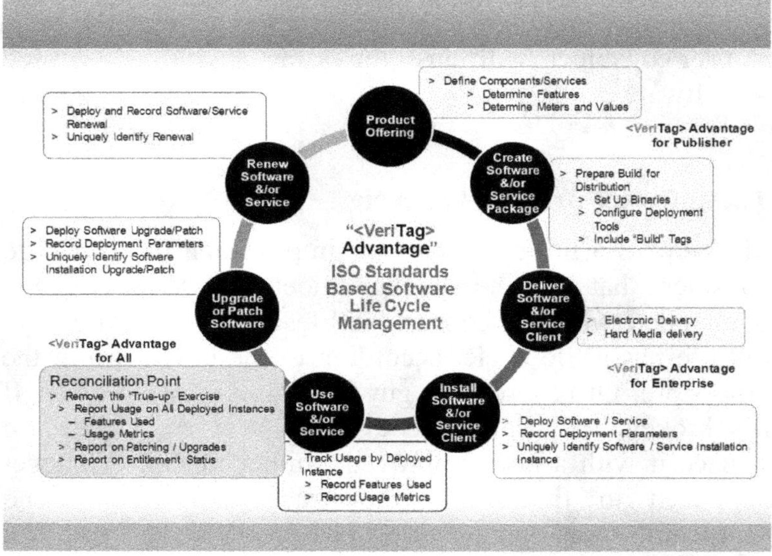

Figure 3: Software/SaaS product life cycle

Figure 3 centres greatly around VeriTag products, but there will be other products appearing over time that can support similar functionality. The life cycle and appropriate points of contact for ISO/IEC 19770 ID tags remain relevant for all supporting tools and products.

Product offering

During this step, usually carried out by product management, software product offerings (licences for use/entitlements) are defined. This involves defining the product components; that is to say the basic configuration, optional or add-on features, meters, suites, etc. At this time, a tool such as VeriTag Publisher (VTP) may be used to define the configuration and the set of ISO/IEC tags associated with each of these components and entitlements.

Once this has been completed, a tool such as VTP, with database functionality, contains the tag prototype information required in order to generate SWID (19770-2) and SWEID (19770-3) tags on demand, either manually or automatically via a web service application programming interface (API) if available.

It may be possible, with an appropriate tag architecture, to create a one-to-one or many-to-one correlation between SWEID tag prototypes and SWID tag prototypes at this point. Doing so will allow the two types of possibly unique tags that are generated later in the life cycle to be associated with each other. This topic is covered in more detail in a later section illustrating the design of tags. If it is possible to create this association, the information generated as a result can be invaluable when deployments and usage are reconciled with entitlements during the product usage cycle.

Create software package and configure the fulfilment infrastructure

As the distribution is built ready to ship to customers, placeholders are created by a SWID creation tool such as VTP. These placeholders will contain the SWID tags that are ultimately generated for inclusion in a distribution that is shipped, either via electronic distribution (ESD) or physical media.

The SWEID tag prototype may also be associated with a unique licence price item at this point. Doing so will allow the generation of a uniquely identifiable SWEID tag when an entitlement is granted as the result of a transaction entitling a user to be licensed to use a software component.

If the software component is tagged with a SWID generated by a SWID prototype that has been associated with the SWEID prototype that generated the SWEID tag for the entitlement, these unique tags may in turn be associated throughout their complete life cycle for management purposes.

Fulfil software and entitlement

At this point in the life cycle, it is possible to inject the SWID tags into the shipped distribution. Using a VeriTag patented process built into VTP, the publisher/OEM has the option to create a uniquely identifiable SWID tag for each shipment, allowing the distribution to be referenced back to a specific business transaction if required.

Alternatively, the publisher may merely create a static build SWID tag that is shipped with all distributions, still enabling the end-user to identify precisely the version of product distribution that was used to install the product which is eventually used within the customer infrastructure.

A publisher/OEM also has the option, using a tool such as VTP, to create and fulfil a SWEID tag that can be used by consumers as a source of truth for their entitlement. This tag may be read and understood by an enterprise software management tool such as VeriTag Enterprise (VTE) for consumer management.

A useful piece of functionality supplied within the currently proposed ISO/IEC 19770-3 draft contains mechanisms that allow a consumer organisation to take a single 'root' entitlement and allocate the entitlement across one or more subsidiary organisations, creating partial entitlements from the original root entitlement.

Install software

Installer scripts and programs that have been integrated with a tool such as VeriTag Writer Suite have the ability to customise the SWID tags for each software installation with a variety of information specific to the installation process. The information, which might include time and date, authorisation information, etc., is in addition to that data supplied in the SWID tag included in the software distribution by the publisher/OEM.

If the end-user environment contains a SWID tag-enabled tool such as VTE, the record of deployment can be updated in the enterprise embedded-software management database for use by the end-user in software management and, ultimately, reconciliation exercises. If the SWID tag has not already been uniquely identified by the software publisher and is a static build SWID tag, a tool such as VTE can serialise each deployed tag uniquely. Additionally, if the publisher has supplied a SWEID tag for the entitlement, the SWEID tag's unique identifier may also be associated with the deployment, allowing ongoing 'true-up' information to be available on a continuous basis, not just at reconciliation time.

When a deployment of software is removed, removal scripts that have been integrated with a tool such as VeriTag Writer Suite can record the removal of the software with the same amount of detail as that recorded during installation. The information is stored and transmitted to the enterprise embedded-software management database, if present, in the end-user environment.

Use software

There is an element within the SWID tag that defines the characteristic of product usage. This element contains information that will allow a SAM tool that is SWID tag enabled to execute algorithms that can measure some level of activity or usage.

Software products that have been integrated with VeriTag Writer Suite runtime libraries can record not only activation and usage data for collection by VTE at any time, but may also optionally use patented technology integrated within VeriTag Writer Suite that can measure incremental usage on a feature-by-feature and/or meter-by-meter basis.

In addition, in the end-user environment, if VTE is installed, a record of software and SaaS usage is maintained regularly within in the VTE software management database for use by the end-user for SAM purposes.

Upgrade or patch software

In much the same fashion as during initial deployment of a product, patching/installer scripts and programs that have been integrated with a tool such as VeriTag Writer Suite have the ability to tag each software installation with a variety of upgrade information specific to the upgrade or patching process, as well as that data supplied in the SWID tag included in the software distribution by the publisher/OEM. Once again, as with the initial installation, each tag may be uniquely identified for management purposes with both the upgrade/patch event as well as the entitlement (tag) that qualifies the upgrade/patch event.

During this step, software that was not previously tagged with information may have its deployments upgraded with newly designed SWID tags and have the information recorded in the VTE (or functionally similar) database, if in use in the end-user environment.

Such a practice allows end-users to revise legacy software products that were released prior to the existence of the ISO/IEC 19770-2:2009 standard such that they may be managed by tag-enabled software life cycle management tools such as VTE in a similar fashion to those newer products being released with this functionality.

Renew software and/or service

Acquiring a renewal via a business transaction of some kind may result in the issuance of a new SWEID tag, which can be associated with previous renewals and even perhaps other entitlements such as licence entitlements. A service can consist possibly of SaaS, maintenance, content for some application (signatures for security issues, mapping updates, document updates, etc.) or possibly combinations thereof.

Reconciliation point

This is the point at which the 'hands clapping' might be achieved. Currently, as only the ISO/IEC 19770-2:2009 SWID tag standard is officially defined by ISO, the reconciliation is very 'right-hand centric' since only deployment information has been enabled by the standard. However, the ISO/IEC 19770-3 entitlement tagging standard defining the SWEID tag is very close behind (the first draft having been completed), which when adopted will enable raw entitlement information management.

At any point in time, as defined by the end-user, a tool such as VTE may report on all tagged and recorded software within the end-user environment. This information may extend to uniquely identified installation events, removal events, product usage and redeployment. By the end of 2011, the tools will be available for both publishers and enterprises to track entitlements using the '-3' standard in anticipation of the official adoption of the proposed standard by ISO.

However, as shown earlier, the exercise of reconciliation, while hopefully being somewhat simplified by the availability of raw information available via the use of SWID and SWEID tags, will still be complex and require judgement calls based on business rules.

Associated life cycles

As I have tried to explain above, the view of software is not simple when considering the product life cycle. To add complexity to the earlier illustration, there are several intersecting life cycles, some depending upon your point of view, provider or consumer perhaps, some depending upon your role. Here are some examples:

- Software product manager – who is concerned only with the annual revenue generated by the licences sold, and therefore the evolution of the product, how the licences are offered and the release schedule, in order to maximise the market.
- Software support and services manager – who is concerned with how much can be made annually from support revenue, how to offer support with as little cost

as possible in a continual stream of ever-changing licensing models that defy understanding or continuity.

- Brand protection manager – who is concerned that all the copies of software in use are:
  - not pirate versions
  - used in compliance with the terms of the licences sold.
- Chief finance officer (CFO) of the enterprise – who has purchased the rights to use the software.
- IT manager – who is deploying the software on behalf of the purchasing enterprise.

For software management to be successful, all of these consumers of software management information must be satisfied.

The product management life cycle

A product manager typically thinks of the product life cycle as outlined in Figure 3. The time line between conception and first release to general access can be months or even years, depending very much upon the characteristics of the market that the product is being sold into. For instance, a security product usually must have a very fast cycle rate, since it is a weapon in the cyberwars and is built to respond rapidly to threats, either anticipated or existing.

A banking application (yawn), once released, may change very slowly. The world's bankers usually have a very conservative attitude towards change (as we have all seen, despite recent economic circumstances) and if an application isn't broken, they want no improvements unless the changes provide a very measurable financial benefit.

Even then, the risk of changes causing some instability sometimes prevents even the smallest evolution from being applied to an existing deployment. I have seen circumstances where existing releases have been in place for several years, and even then only the need for an upgrade due to unsupported or worn-out hardware has forced the installation of new versions of software.

So what is the product manager looking for in information provided by software management? This is marketing information. You might think such information can be gathered from sales information, but how licences are sold does not necessarily match how products are used. Here is the concept of needing two-handed clapping again. Product managers need to understand usage trends in order to blend those trends with anticipated future requirements. Past usage trends may help as predictors of the future, although I once worked with a sales vice-president who claimed that product managers who were passionate about past usage trends were like automobile drivers navigating a journey by looking in the rear-view mirror!

The critical points for software management information in this life cycle come at the stage where the pricing and licensing decisions and designs are made. If the licence offerings are such that the business value to the consumer of the software for each offering can be measured, then sooner or later the consumer will select an alternative. Therefore, if the usage of the software in real-world terms cannot be reconciled with the cost of the licence and maintenance of the software or service, the consumer is at a disadvantage. If this information is not available from publisher A, but is available from publisher B, then even if A's product shows some functional advantage over B's product, a consumer (especially our banker!) will likely choose B.

Let me give you an illustration of what I mean here. Consider the software publisher who sells the product based on a meter that is derived from the size of the CPU (model, cores, clock speed or some other measure). Unless there is a clear measurement of 'real work' throughput in the application of the software, how can the consumer possibly understand the business benefit of purchasing licences this way?

Let's look at my friend, Hans, who ran a small private railway in Switzerland. His railway transported people up 10 km of track to a mountain resort. Each time, his train travelled at a certain speed owing to track conditions, and he could only put a finite number of carriages on his train because the platform length of each station limited the number of carriages that could be loaded and unloaded simultaneously. Now, while it is very clear that had he been able to purchase a locomotive of twice the power, theoretically his train would run faster or could carry more passengers at the same speed, but real-world constraints prevented that. Thus charging passengers more for travelling on a train powered by a more powerful locomotive was not an option.

In a similar fashion, our software consumer must have a way of measuring the value in a simple fashion; that is to say, the value of the software in business terms, i.e. the effective use as well as throughput of the application over an appropriate period of time.

This ability is part of the role that should be played by software management, and it is the responsibility of the product manager to ensure that these measurements are possible from any deployment of the software. The licensed offering must be measurable in terms of functionality and meter.

This factor becomes even more important in the virtual machine (VM) world, where the separation of software from the hardware platform is becoming more distant as VMs evolve.

The software support life cycle

I have another friend, let's call him Steve, who is a sales engineer (SE) for a very large software publisher. He is located in Detroit and covers a large area helping to support and comfort several significant enterprise software users in the region. Steve is the kind of fellow who stands up in the middle of the global quarterly earnings report and asks the CEO, 'If we are doing so well, how come we can't afford to develop better, or even *any*, tools for our customers to manage the software we sell them?'

Steve is on the front line daily with his customers, dealing with 'out of band' problems as well as the normal events in the software life cycle such as a 'true-up'.

Steve's life cycle starts with a new product release and rotates through renewal cycles.

Tag life cycles

The SWID and SWEID tags have their own life cycles. Depending upon how the tags are used (more on this topic late), these cycles start and stop at different parts of the software product life cycle, but intersect at well-defined points.

Critical measurements required for software asset management

Ultimately, functionality exploiting the ISO/IEC 19770-3 SWEID standards currently under development will be included in the software management process. The standard approval is scheduled for late in 2011 or early in 2012.

When corresponding deployments are measured in order to match against entitlements for any given product, licence model or business rules for product usage, there are frequent changes from release to release. Therefore, it is important to understand the version and release date for each product deployment, since an entitlement for one release may not be valid for another as the business rules governing the deployment may be different. There are also cases where a single product may be licensed in multiple ways. An example of this situation could be that a single product might be offered in, say, France and Belgium; both are French language versions, but are either priced very differently or metered very differently.

In this situation, a deployment report could look identical for the two different versions of the product, since the functional model is the same for each. However, the entitlement purchases may be different for each and therefore this has an impact on the compliance assessment.

CHAPTER 2: CURRENT APPROACHES IN BOTH PROCESS AND TECHNOLOGY

The people

I am reluctant to dwell in detail on the topic of software management, especially the asset management aspect, for risk of sounding more like a critic and detractor than a promoter of technology. The truth is, the art of software management thus far has very much been exactly that; 'art'.

As with all art, the success of many of the tools has very much relied upon the artists handling them and there are some very fine practitioners in the field today. Again, at the risk of alienating people for whom I have a great deal of respect, I am not going to mention names specifically.

Other than my SE friend, Steve, that is, whom I mentioned earlier. Yes, some of the finest practitioners of the art are the loyal SEs who are out in the field helping customers. I should mention that most if not all, including Steve, of the SEs I have known have been loyal to both customers and employers, since they realise that the long-term relationships that they have built with their customers on behalf of their company are fragile and worth sustaining for the benefit of both sides.

No, I have never been an SE, plus I know several third-party audit specialists who might disagree with me, but several years of working with these SEs have revealed no exceptions that would change my point of view.

The process

The basic principle is exactly as I have mentioned earlier: the enforcement of the balance of consumption with entitlement. There are two extremes in achieving this enforcement.

Hard enforcement

This is really the practice of restraining the use of software and services with some technology that cuts off usage beyond a certain pre-agreed threshold that is defined by the maximum entitlement. Depending upon the licensing model, such enforcement can either be very simple or extremely complex. At the extreme, hard enforcement can constrain usage to the location, the time and perhaps even the user, to rules as defined in a licence agreement.

The trick often is for the software or service to be aware of the context that it is running within in order to provide enforcement. If the constraint is the number of CPUs then the software enforcement mechanisms must have a way of measuring this metric (I have not made any judgement here as to whether this is a sensible meter of course!).

Why do we need hard enforcement? The basic premise is, of course, that potential users of such products have no desire to conform to the licence agreement and their behaviour cannot be policed in any other way. In general, from my experience, most enterprise software users do not fall into this category.

However, there are a couple of environments where this might be a valid judgement:

1 The anonymous user – perhaps a small business user buys software off the shelf as a boxed product in a store. This user perhaps has no desire for any relationship with the software supplier and regards the product as a commodity for exploitation.
2 Users in certain geographies – there are regions in the world where: a) intellectual property (IP) is not valued or held in high economic regard, and b) the governing bodies have few rules to protect IP and probably have no enforcement of any rules that might exist.

The climate is changing though. As more regions that originally were purely at the consumption end of IP commerce now become inventors in their own right, there is an increasing awareness that their own IP must be protected and attitudes are changing.

Many enterprise software vendors are moving away from this form of enforcement.

A story comes to mind where this move was greeted with enthusiasm by a Swiss Bank that was upgrading its servers late on one Saturday night. Since this was a quiet time in the global weekly business cycle, the IT department elected to upgrade to new hardware in a quick overnight, well-planned upgrade session. The bank's IT team even practised the upgrade using a test machine during normal working hours to ensure that the window, four hours, was sufficient to shut down, perform an upgrade and restart the system. It seemed that everything could be achieved easily in three hours, maybe even faster, since the test system was not as powerful as the new system being installed. With such preparation, all went well, right?

Wrong! When the new system came up, the US-developed application realised that it was now running on a more powerful platform and that the licence key was not valid for a platform of this level of performance. Three hours out of four gone, no time to restore the original hardware… panic at 3 am in Zurich!

Luckily (or not, depending upon who you were), the software vendor had an SE on site from the Germany office. He surely had keys available to him, either in Germany or in the US? Unfortunately, this was not the case. The US software vendor had recently been acquired and thus their systems and support were in the middle of the integration transition. This is where the 'people magic' kicked in. The SE was able to call a head-office licensing expert in California, with whom he had a personal relationship, on his cell phone. The expert was at a baseball game in San Francisco (6 pm Pacific Time), but fortunately had a laptop in his car in the parking lot. He ran out to his car and generated a new key across the Web. He then e-mailed it off to Zurich and went back into the ball park to watch the rest of the game. By 3.15 am Zurich time, the application was starting itself up happily on the new key. All the necessary licensing paperwork between the bank and the publisher was taken care of after the fact.

Believe it or not, there are flip sides to this story. A new agreement was being made for a public utility in the southern US. A new set of products to replace older, hard-enforced products was being offered. Suddenly, on realising that hard enforcement was no longer in place on the newer product set, the chief information officer (CIO) of the utility baulked at the deal. The premise for his reluctance? He was concerned that he could no longer control indiscriminate deployment of the product set by his IT managers.

Should this CIO rely upon hard enforcement of the product to police his own management team? Should the CIO and his team not have adequate management processes in place to prevent this from occurring?

In the absence of adequate, hopefully cross-vendor, software management tools, maybe this was the CIO's only affordable option.

The bottom-line message here is: other than providing more information and allowing proactive software, and thus key, management, ISO/IEC 19770 standards provide nothing in the way of improved hard enforcement functionality.

Soft enforcement

So called because there may not be any immediate impact for exceeding a licence agreement or entitlement limits, the impact remains, however deferred, because the balance between entitlement and usage must remain in place at all times.

Soft enforcement is very hard to manage without a good set of tools for managing usage as well as an equally efficient set of tools for managing licences and entitlements. Theoretically, the management processes are easier to execute, though no less rigorous than processes for managing hard-enforced tools. Since there is no requirement for key management, reporting and tracking are the order of the day.

Increased use of the Cloud introduces shifts in paradigm also. The traditional licensing models are shifting towards the concept of user provisioning. This is not all bad, since licensing can also be shifted perhaps towards the utility model. This requires similar processes, techniques and technology across both services and licensing, something that the ISO/IEC 19770 standards can leverage.

Let me explain what I mean by utility model. Those of you using water in the City of Surrey in British Columbia, Canada, may not need an explanation. For many years, houses have not had metered water usage in this location. Having spent some considerable time in BC, I can understand in some ways why this was the case at the outset. There is so much water falling out of the sky in BC throughout the year that the thought of actually having to measure consumption once the water service was available to households was not a consideration.

I moved to California, Marin County, in 1981 and soon realised that water was a precious commodity in this region. In Santa Cruz, where I live now, there are frequent water usage restrictions during the summer (which starts on 4 January and ends on 23 December, in order to allow for a white Christmas!). This may seem like a slight exaggeration, but there are times when January has had no rain and temperatures in the 80s Fahrenheit. Which means the snow pack, which we rely on in California (a great deal of which can be classified as desert) for our water given the lack of natural lakes full of fresh water, does not always carry enough to satisfy our state's thirst.

Some believe that fresh water will be the strategic commodity of the future, rather than oil, and Canada will be one of the main sources for the world. Hence, the City of Surrey is now mandating meters in each household and will be measuring, and billing for, water on a usage, or utility, basis going forward.

As the City of Surrey puts it, 'Metering water in a household helps determine how much a family uses, and might even change some habits. Metering is also an opportunity to save money on the utility bill.'

Many, although not all, consumers of software would like to purchase their software in the same fashion.

There is a design house in Silicon Valley that uses computer-aided design (CAD) software (who doesn't these days?) and their cycle of usage over the year varies. At one point in the year they have 500 concurrent workstations actively running the CAD applications. At other times, when the products are through the design cycle and into manufacture, they are using many fewer workstations. However, in order to support this habit, since the CAD software publisher only offers perpetual licences sold by the seat, the design house has to purchase and maintain 500 licences for year-round use. Of course, they would much rather just pay for use on a utility basis – the utility model – and who knows, they might even change some work habits!

CHAPTER 3: WHAT IS ISO/IEC 19770?

Oh no! Not another standard!

It may be apparent that I have avoided using the term SAM to a large extent in this book. This is deliberate on my part since, as I have mentioned earlier, I regard SAM as only one component of software life cycle management, a component largely in the domain of the software consumer.

While ISO/IEC 19770 came about largely as a result of the problems faced by SAM practitioners, from my own point of view the impact of the standards is greater and their use can benefit many aspects of the software life cycle. I hope that, overall, this book starts to show this and allows the reader to look for further benefits outside the SAM domain.

There are those, quite correctly, that make the point that SAM has been around for many years and, while not necessarily constituting a roaring success, the tools in use allow for the most part a satisfactory level of management. There are others that maintain, possibly also equally correctly, that SAM is more black magic than it is science.

So given common arguments against forming standards, such as 'standards constrain innovation' or 'standards evolve as a result of common practices and are not predefined', why attempt to introduce a proposed set of standards that may be used for SAM?

Earlier I spoke of the 'two-handed clapping' metaphor where software usage is matched against entitlement. If you re-examine my metaphor in the context of past entitlement and SAM tool technologies, you will notice:

1 There has never been any agreement between those building tools to detect product presence and/or usage and software publisher/OEMs on the validity of the information derived and reported upon by these tools.
2 The process of reconciliation, especially for audit purposes, always requires the participation of the publisher/OEM in order to validate any entitlement information used as part of the reconciliation process against product usage.

In defining this standard, for the first time, publishers/OEMs are explicitly agreeing to:

1 a quantitative definition of software product structure and components, thus defining the basic elements required from inventory management that are needed for software life cycle management;
2 a quantitative definition of an entitlement that may be unambiguously used in attempting to understand the terms of software and/or service use.

If for no other reason, these two pieces of functionality provided by the standard form the foundation for my goal as stated in the introduction to this book:

Quantifying the value delivered by software/SaaS and removing the 'us versus them' framework between publisher and customer in enterprise software commerce.

In addition, the standards relate to all aspects of the software life cycle with co-operation between all parties involved, both on the publisher side and the consumer side. The standards also allow participation of third parties, such as OEMs and third-party independent software vendors (ISVs), in the life cycle process.

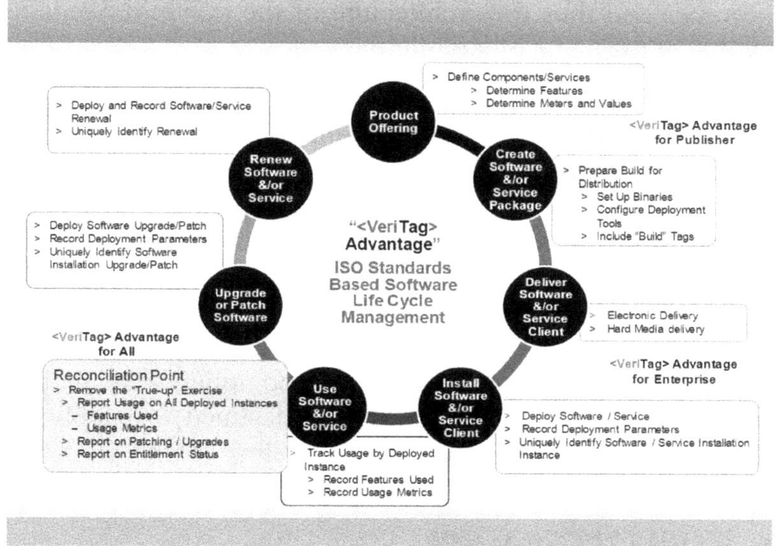

Figure 4: Software/SaaS product life cycle

This very powerful paradigm enables a coherent approach to software (and service) life cycle management that has never been possible before.

A quick view of the ISO/IEC 19770 standard

Overview

The home of the ISO/IEC 19770 standard can be found at *www.19770.org*. This is the website for the working group known as ISO/IEC JTC1 SC7 WG21.

The standard consists of multiple parts, currently five, although it is not clear at any particular time which of all the parts are actively being worked upon. The reason I say currently is that it seems that as we all learn more about the science of this standard, the more complex the topic becomes and thus the architecture of the standard needs to evolve in the name of simplicity.

Part one defines the processes of SAM. The second defines software product and component identification and is intended to support the processes defined in the first part. The third part identifies entitlements, which are ultimately balanced against software usage when attempting to ensure that what is entitled is actually used; no more, no less. The fourth is once again about processes, and attempts to break down the processes in the first part in a tiered fashion in order to make multiple levels of compliance available. There is also a fifth project that is destined to supply an overall introduction and glossary for ISO/IEC SAM standards:

- **ISO/IEC 19770-1:2006**
  - SAM best practices
- **ISO/IEC 19770-2:2009**
  - Software ID tagging standard
- **ISO/IEC 19770-3 (under development)**
  - Software entitlements tagging standard
- **ISO/IEC 19770-4 (under development)**
  - Phased approach to adoption of -1 best practices
- **ISO/IEC 19770-5 (under development)**
  - Glossary for the overall standard.

ISO/IEC 19770-1:2006

There are two parts to this standard:

1 This contains the processes as applied to the SAM control environment, including those specific to

corporate governance, organisational roles and responsibilities, policies and procedures, and finally assurance of competence with respect to SAM.

2 This contains the processes of SAM planning and implementation, together with the monitoring and evolution/improvement of SAM.

There are a total of 27 process areas divided into the categories listed above.

ISO/IEC 19770-2:2009

This portion of the standards, the focal point of this book, defines the structure of SWID tags. Quoting from the standard:

> The software identification tag is an XML file containing identification and management information about a software product, which is installed onto a computing device together with the software product. The tag may be created as part of the installation process, or added later for software already installed without tags. However, it is expected more commonly that the tag will be created when the software product is originally developed, and then be distributed and installed together with the software product.

The goal of the SWID tag standard is to provide information about a software installation that:

- is cross-platform
- is cross-publisher
- provides application lineage
- provides an application footprint
- has standard structure
- uses XML-based data
- is easily discovered
- is authoritative and accurate.

ISO/IEC 19770-3 (under development)

ISO/IEC 19770-3 will provide a software life cycle management data standard for SWEID tags that:

- is cross-platform
- is cross-publisher
- has a direct link to SWID tags
- has licence metrics defined
- has standard structure
- uses XML-based data
- is easily incorporated into tools
- automates compliance.

The goals are all very laudable, but rather idealistic in the real world. For instance, in some cases it might be possible to link SWEID tags with SWID tags. However, as explained in an earlier chapter, the rules of business and the delicate balance of compliance may obscure these mappings.

In step with this wrinkle, I am not convinced that automated compliance will ever be achievable, although in some cases the possibility of reaching an approximation with automated processes is greater.

ISO/IEC 19770-4 (under development)

This is the most elusive of the standards and proposes a multi-tiered approach to ISO/IEC 19770-1:2006. The work probably should not be considered a new standard, i.e. -4, but more appropriately a restructuring of -1. The tiers proposed are:

- Tier One – Trustworthy Data – building an accurate inventory of all items to be managed

- Tier Two – Practical Management – implementing basic management processes and controls
- Tier Three – Operational Integration – implementing SAM as a part of daily operations
- Tier Four – Full ISO Conformance – ensuring SAM can become a strategic enabler to business.

Below is an overview of the achievements to date:

- **May 2006**: ISO releases first SAM processes standards – ISO/IEC 19770 Part 1 – Processes.
- **October 2007**: Extensive industry survey by ISO to understand market needs for SAM standards.
- **March 2008**: ISO receives submissions proposing stages for evolutionary adoption of SAM.
- **May 2008**: Berlin meeting of ISO/IEC Working Group 21 (ISO/IEC JTC 1/SC 7/WG 21). When the results were released, they showed strong market demand for Tiers.
- **May 2009**: Hyderabad meeting of Working Group 21 (ISO reference as above) gave:
    - agreement to base stages upon submitted and tested tiers
    - agreement to base draft staged SAM standard on processes and format of 19770 Part 1.
- **October 2009**: Reading (UK) ISO/IEC Working Group for SAM (ISO/IEC JTC 1/SC 7/WG 21) created an Other Working Group (OWG):
    - It was to develop the ISO/IEC 19770-4 standard with the goal to agree its normative text at the Niigata Plenary.

- o David Phillips, of SAM leaders, was appointed as the convener of the (formerly designated 19770-4) Staged SAM OWG.
- o The OWG convened with 12 SAM industry professionals in attendance.

- **February 2010**: New work item for Part 4 is circulated by ISO for worldwide member-body voting.
- **April 2010**: New work item is passed for worldwide member-body voting.
- **September 2010**: Acting on the supporting resolution of the ISO/IEC Technical Committee on Software and Systems Engineering (ISO/IEC JTC1/SC7), work is completed on a revision of the 19770-1:2006 standard, as described above.

The OWG successfully submitted all working document materials on time to SC7 Interim meeting in Gaithersburg MD, USA in November 2010. The next step is a CD-ROM release of the standards document and several annexes providing guidance requested in industry trials.

More recently, as part of the evangelism of ISO/IEC 19770-1, the first tiered document, which is the revision of the original standard, has been circulated for review by Working Group 21. The revision work has been led by ISO/IEC JTC1/SC7/WG21 Convener, David Bicket, and a group that is drawn upon from all over the world.

A good place to see the latest status of this work is at *www.19770.org/*.

CHAPTER 4: INTRODUCTION TO THE SWID TAG

It is important to understand that classic tagging only indicates the raw functional model deployment in general. Therefore it may offer only part of the business rules of deployment in many cases since the overall licensing model, which may go beyond simple functionality, may not be detectable.

ISO/IEC 19770-2 software ID tag functionality

This part of ISO/IEC 19770 was developed in order to provide a software data standard for software/software component tagging. This is the process by which digital identification (SWID tag) is made to contain information about a given software configuration and the items or components it contains, so as to best facilitate deployed software identification and management.

Significant standardisation in SWID tag content makes software life cycle management practices more efficient, consistent and straightforward. Certifiable systematic software tagging practices also allow information technology professionals and others to place reliance on the adequacy of these practices and the consequences of standardised tagging benefits all parties involved in software life cycle management.

Operational breakdown

SWID tag business functions

SWID tag creation

- Create SWID tag to identify software and origin, with creators furnishing most mandatory SWID tag elements.
- Create optional SWID tag elements to facilitate identification and software life cycle management.
- Create SWID tag when none is provided by manufacturer, with modifiers or consumers furnishing SWID tag data in such an instance.

SWID tag modification

- Modify SWID tag information, particularly incomplete mandatory SWID tag elements.
- Provide additional SWID tag information, such as those identity elements pertaining to release management.
- Ensure consistent and uniform values in SWID tag data.

SWID tag consumption

- Implement SWID tag information for software life cycle management purposes.
- Rely on SWID tag information as being in compliance with ISO standards.

SWID tag business roles

SWID tag creators

The creators are software manufacturers, ISVs, software publishers and line-of-business application developers. The benefits from standardisation in software tagging practices for these parties include, but are not limited to, the following:

1. The end-installation immediately recognises who created the software being installed.
2. If the SWID tag creator resolves to allow a reseller, OEM customer or distributor to change the software identification information, the SWID tag creator can specify exactly what can and cannot be changed in the SWID tag and thus work to ensure consistency in software identification.
3. By making software easier to identify and potentially simple to correlate to software licences, the SWID tag creator benefits from SWID tag consumers' increased awareness of licence compliance issues (consumers are more likely to purchase additional software items from software manufacturers, publishers and vendors should they find themselves out of compliance).
4. By defining SWID tags as early in the software life cycle as possible, projects for software under development become focused on the right tools and technology to meet the requirements specified for target languages and platforms.
5. Manufacturers, publishers and vendors thus make software that is easy to identify, install and use.

Example SWID tag creators include:

- **Software manufacturers**: a SWID tag is frequently created when the manufacturer builds software. Subsequently, the SWID tag and product are shipped together. Software may be dispatched directly to the consumer, a publisher or both. For this reason, arrangements have to be pre-planned as to who creates the SWID tag and who defines the software origins. It is possible that this process may have mixed ownership as it depends upon the channel used for software distribution.
- **Independent software vendors**: similar to the manufacturer in the tagging life cycle role, the independent software vendor building and publishing proprietary software must include, as part of the release process, the creation of a SWID tag to ship with media.
- **Software publishers**: when software is developed by another organisation and then shipped for publication, the publisher can create a SWID tag during the packing process to include in the media.
- **Line-of-business application developers**: in-house application developers can also create SWID tags to include in their media.
- **Distributors, repackagers, value-added resellers**: parties that distribute software that was received without standardised SWID tags may add them so as to accommodate the needs of their end-users.
- **Release publishers**: when a software package does not include a standardised SWID tag, end-users are encouraged to create and embed their own SWID tag so as to conform to ISO/IEC 19770-1 SAM processes.

Tag creation mechanisms

A SWID tag can be conceived and created at any time, and this process is not necessarily part of the engineering process for the software product to be tagged.

In their simplest form, tags may be created as a single object (a single instance of a software ID tag) per software component and the tag is then bundled with the distribution at distribution build time. The tag may then exist, unaltered, for its entire lifetime and remain forever static in content. Such practice, while useful, does not take full advantage of the abilities that the SWID tag enables by leveraging the attributes (elements) that a SWID tag contains.

Use of VTP enables a SWID tag to have some attributes injected at creation time, prior to the signing of the SWID tag that may eventually be used to track the life cycle of the deployed software that the SWID is installed with. Examples of these attributes are as follows:

- Serial_number – allows each instance of a generated SWID to be uniquely identified and thus indexed back to the transaction that created it. Such a transaction might include the generation of a licence for use of the software component being tagged. This value, in combination with the software_licensor_alias attribute might possibly be used at reconciliation time in order to help verify the exact details of the licence status of the deployment. Another kind of transaction may be the generation of an ESD distribution from an identifiable ESD delivery system that can be included in the data_source element, enabling reconciliation of a distribution with a distribution generation, and thus the publisher business transaction that enabled the distribution delivery.

- SKU – may be the stock-keeping unit (SKU) for the licence generated (either from the publisher's ESD delivery system or perhaps the enterprise resource planning (ERP) system); again, in combination with the software_licensor_alias attribute it might possibly be used at reconciliation time in order to help verify the exact details of the licence status of the deployment.

The SWID tags are signed and certified in real time by a tool such as VTP. Appropriate integration of VTP into the software publisher/SWID tag creator's infrastructure would be required to achieve this.

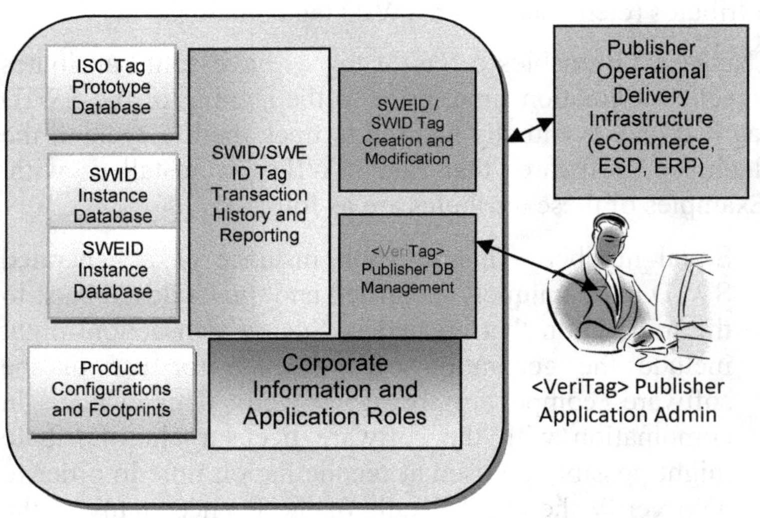

Figure 5: VeriTag Publisher application

SWID tag modifiers

Tags are modified by SAM and other software life cycle management tool providers, deployment tool providers, software resellers, value-added resellers, republishers, packagers and release publishers. The benefits from standardisation in software tagging practices for these parties include, but are not limited to, the following:

1 SWID tag modifiers are able to expect consistent and uniform values in SWID tag data.
2 Products released by SAM and other software life cycle management tool providers and deployment tool providers can more easily discover mandatory software tag information by virtue of the implementation of standardised location and formatting of SWID tag data.
3 Products released by SAM and other software life cycle management tool providers and deployment tool providers are able to utilise SWID tag data to reconcile an application from discovery information.
4 Products released by SAM and other software life cycle management tool providers and deployment tool providers are able to utilise SWID tag data to distinguish differences between licensed and unlicensed applications.
5 Products released by SAM and other software life cycle management tool providers and deployment tool providers are better able to determine from SWID tag data whether or not an application should be installed on a particular platform or computer system.
6 SAM and other software life cycle management tool providers and deployment tool providers are able to free more proprietary resources to enhance best practices and improve product lines by virtue of improvements made in software identification via tagging standardisation.

7 SWID tag information is used to assist in the automation of the packaging of an application for distribution.
8 Distributors, repackagers and resellers can more easily determine if a particular SWID tag needs modification by having quicker access to the requisite information.
9 Distributors, repackagers and resellers can ensure that SWID tag creators have properly tagged their software.

Examples of SWID tag modifiers include:

- distributors
- software resellers
- value-added resellers
- republishers
- packagers
- sam tool providers
- deployment tool providers
- release publishers.

SWID tag consumers

Tag consumers include SAM owners, IT support professionals and end-users of a given software configuration item. The benefits from standardisation in software tagging practices for these parties include, but are not limited to, the following:

1 Asset publishers, professionals and end-users are able to rely on software products as compliant with industry-standard identification mechanisms.
2 Standardised tagging can improve inventory identification, thereby enhancing the ability to provide details regarding a given software product's origination,

modification and dependencies upon other software products and operating system platforms.

3 Standardised tagging improves SAM and other software life cycle management and eases compliance auditing by shifting some of the work of reconciling software inventory to the publishers and by enhancing processes of reconciling software use entitlements and installation data.

4 Standardised tagging across multiple computing and operating system platforms brings order and consistency to identifying what is installed on a given computing device.

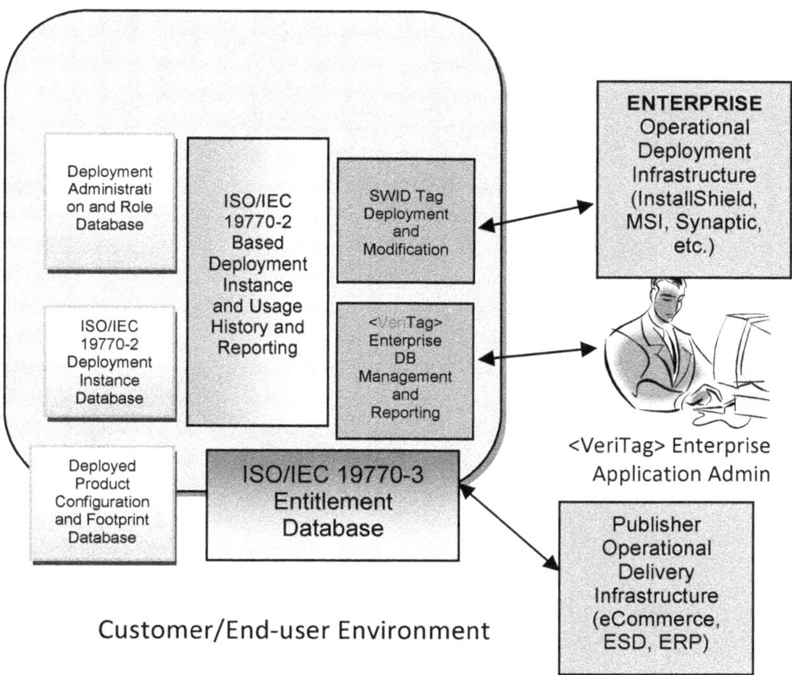

Figure 6: VeriTag Enterprise application

CHAPTER 5: IMPLEMENTATION OF THE ISO/IEC 19770-2 PROCESS

ISO/IEC 19770 general guidelines

Consistency among data types

Data input into tagging fields must maintain consistencies that optimise the software detection processes for discovery tools, SAM and other software life cycle management owners alike. For example, it is recommended that, if possible, software manufacturers should maintain consistency in the manufacturer name field within any given product line. Although this document does not require consistency in the manufacturer name field for operating systems, uniformity is strongly urged.

Pre-manufactured media

Acknowledging that some resellers may only ship pre-manufactured media and therefore find tag modification difficult or impossible, this document proposes three possible implementation alternatives to allow for, or preclude the necessity of, reseller tag modification:

- Download a tag separately from the media – an alternative that requires a manual step from the reseller to get the correct tag from the manufacturer and to modify it.
- Allocate modification to the software manufacturer, each individual reseller's tags preconfigured with the relevant information specific to that reseller.

- Implement a tag from the manufacturer that is generic enough to preclude the necessity of modification.

Languages

Acknowledging that many manufacturers produce software with specific builds that are dependent on language and that many others produce software with one build that implements add-on language packs, this document does not require that tagging methods allow for the recognition of different language versions for the same product. Consistent categorisation of the type of language solution employed is, however, strongly encouraged.

Tag installation

It is recommended that SWID tags should be routinely embedded into software installers so as to distinguish unapproved versions of a product from approved versions via the presence/absence of a manufacturer's proprietary tag elements.

Unique identification

For purposes of uniqueness, tag creators must create a globally unique identifier (GUID) to assign to each particular piece of software's SWID tag. The value of the GUID should be exclusive to a particular release of software. The GUID can be used to reference a tag in other, related tags. TagVault.org managed tags allow the assignment of a unique GUID across the TagVault domain.

The cross-referencing capabilities of a GUID include, but are not limited to:

- the creation of a supported platforms list in which software vendors can list supported platform unique identifiers in the SWID tag so as to specify operating system compatibilities;
- direct reference of parent-child relationships via the specification of the parent SWID tag for software packages;
- explicit definitions of dependencies by direct references to the GUIDs of dependent software;
- identification of upgrade software as such and specifications for allowed upgrade packages;
- reference from executable software configuration items to corresponding SWID tags via embedded identifiers within the former.

Basic process

The sequence of applying tags consists of multiple steps. For each product requiring tagging, analyse as follows:

- Understand the deployment/functional model.
- Design the tag(s) to describe the functional components of the deployment model.

For each deployment to be tagged:

- Create the tagging directories.
- Deploy tag appropriate to the deployment/functional model.

Understanding the deployment/functional model

Simple classic model

The deployment can be a simple set of binaries that provides a single set of functionality that is not configurable.

Classic Simple Component Tag

- Unique_ID (serial_number, Creator Specific)
- Fulfillment_ID (Tag Specific)
- Entitlement required indicator
- Product Title
- Product Version
- Software Creator
- Software Licensor
- Software Identifier
- Tag Creator (Registration ID for publisher)
- *Optional Elements*
  - *– Level 2 U.S. GSA/DoD SAM Certification Elements*
  - *Non required elements*
- *(Extended Elements)*

Figure 7: Classic tag

In this case, the deployment can be labelled with a single classic tag in two locations:

- root location of the application
- ISO/IEC 19770-2 proposed standard location.

Details of each are described below.

Complex classic model

In the case where there may be add-ons in the deployment model, there are tags for each component, where the build tag can describe the 'base component' and then component tags describe each component.

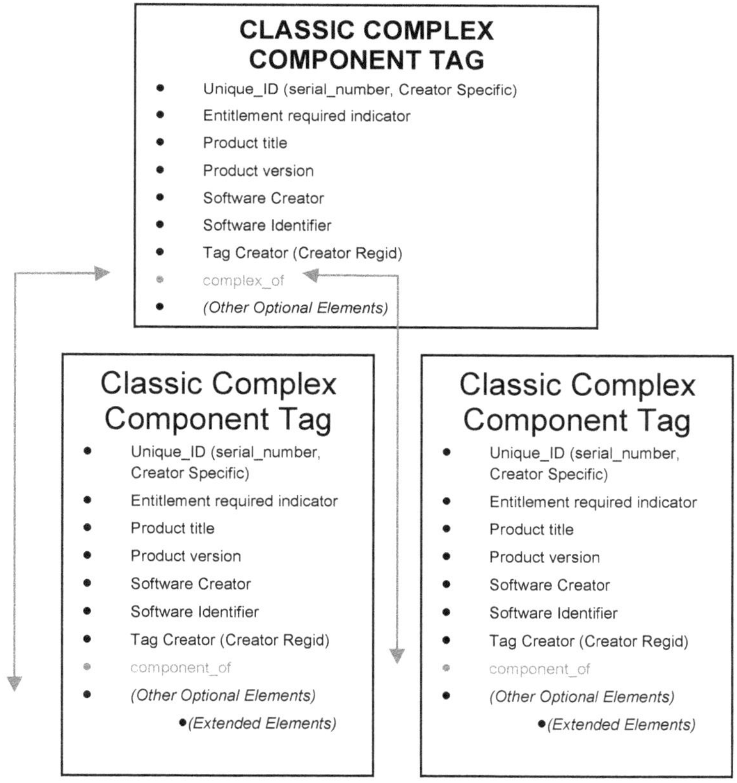

Figure 8: Classic complex tag

If the entire available functionality is installed as a single deployment, then the build tag can describe the deployment. If the additional functionality is achieved by adding new components to the base component, then each component tag can describe the additional deployment.

The presence of any tag does not imply that the software that is tagged is in use. If there are rules for measuring activity, these rules can be derived from the optional usage element, if it is included in the tag.

Attribute/element groups

In the case where attributes may need protection, the attributes are grouped by owner (either a creator or modifier) and the group is signed. In the above example, for instance, all mandatory elements plus either the 'component list' or 'component of' elements might form a group for signing. There may be other elements that do not require protection in any tag generated and these can be formed within the tag at the same time as the signed group by the tag generation mechanism.

Designing the tags to match the functional deployment model

Tag identification

The functionality of an IEC/ISO 19770-2 tag is such that each tag can be identifiable as unique (*see serial_number below in the section on tag optional elements*).

In order to achieve this, there is a preference for a central clearing house that assigns, at minimum, a unique identifier for each tag generated that is identified in the ISO proposed standard as serial_number.

The tag container

The tag container, or file, must also conform to specific parameters. The proposed ISO standard is as follows:

> The name of a software tag must be unique and align with the following structure: <product_title>-<serial_number>.swtag. The components of the tag filename are identity elements required of all software tags. The .swtag file extension can be used for all software tags. This naming scheme allows for multiple software tags to be applied to the same product, thereby providing support for upgrades and audit capabilities.
>
> If a software configuration item is installed for a specific user, a suffix containing user identification information (e.g. 'userID') should be used to differentiate unique installations. An example name in such an instance would be <product_title>-<serial_number>-<userID>.swtag.

An application, such as VTP, must generate digitally signed tag files as part of the process.

The digital signature can be generated uniquely based upon pre-selected criteria, e.g. by publisher or by tag attribute, or a combination of attributes. This functionality can allow verification of tags in a customised fashion.

The clearing house can provide additional services such as:

- providing tag information and contents by tag attribute
- providing other management facilities on a per tag or tag provider basis.

Indicating the presence of an application deployment

The detection of a deployment may vary depending upon the deployment measurement tool.

Create the tagging directories

ISO/IEC 19770-2 standard tagging location

Table 1: Tagging directories

Windows	%ALLUSERPROFILE%\Application Data**<Company>**\ISO-19770
Apple Macintosh, Unix and Linux	Users/Shared/**<Company>**/ISO-19770

The above is the ISO-defined root location.

The field 'Company' can use a unique corporate identifier as assigned by the clearing house, in much the same way as a DNS domain name is assigned. The 'Company' may be chosen by the requestor and maintained as unique by the clearing house. The identifier field may also use the 10-digit IBEI/ISO16372 standard, or the Standard and Poor's, Dun and Bradstreet, etc. identifiers, and be assigned by the clearing house.

Root location of the application

A single classic tag should also be deployed in the top-level directory of the application directory in case it is located on removable media.

This has to be determined by research on the product. This is usually some logical location that is defined as a global environment variable in the installation machine.

CHAPTER 6: THE ISO/IEC 19770-2 SWID TAG DATA FUNDAMENTALS

software_identification_tag	
id	**Element ID Type**
software_identification_tag	SoftwareIdentificationTagComplexType

SoftwareIdentificationTagComplexType	
id	**Element ID Type**
entitlement_required_indicator	Boolean
product_title	Token
product_version	ProductVersionComplexType
software_creator	EntityComplexType
software_licensor	EntityComplexType
software_id	SoftwareidComplexType
tag_creator	EntityComplexType
abstract	AbstractComplexType
component_of	ListOfSoftwareidsComplexType
complex_of	ListOfSoftwareidsComplexType
data_source	Token
dependency	ListOfSoftwareidsComplexType
elements_owner	ElementsOwnerComplexType
installation_details	InstallationDetailsComplexType
keywords	KeywordsComplexType
license_linkage	LicenseLinkageComplexType
package_footprint	PackageFootprintComplexType
packager	PackagerComplexType
product_category	CategoryComplexType
product_family	Token
product_id	Token
release_date	DateTime
release_id	Token
release_package	ReleaseComplexType
release_rollout	ReleaseComplexType
release_verification	ReleaseComplexType
serial_number	Token
sku	Token
software_creator_alias	EntityDataComplexType
software_licensor_alias	EntityDataComplexType
supported_languages	SupportedLanguagesComplexType
tag_creator_alias	EntityDataComplexType
tag_creator_copyright	TagCreatorCopyrightComplexType
tag_version	TagVersionComplexType
upgrade_for	UpgradeForComplexType
usage_identifier	UsageComplexType
validation	ValidationComplexType
Signature	SignatureType
extended_information	ExtendedInformationComplexType

Figure 9: ISO/IEC 19770-2 tag elements

Although derived from actual use and application of the standard in my own experience, the section below does not stand alone in providing complete information on SWID content and structure. I recommend that as you read through this, you refer to the official standards document, 'Information technology – Software asset management – Part 2: Software identification tag', ISO/IEC 19770-2:2009(E).

ISO/IEC 19770-2 mandatory tag elements

As described earlier, there should be a tag designed for each software component or licensable function. In order to comply with basic ISO/IEC 19770-2 standards, the following elements must be included.

Entitlement required indicator

SoftwareIdentificationComplexType	
Id	ID
entitlement_required_indicatior	Boolean

Figure 10: Entitlement required indicator

This element is a Boolean tag that indicates if an entitlement must match up against this item in order for a software reconciliation to be considered successful.

Open source software, for example, may not require an entitlement in the reconciliation process to be legally installed and used. This does not mean that the software does not have an entitlement; simply that it does not need an entitlement specified for the reconciliation to be complete.

This provides the ability for software life cycle managers to manage by exception and focus only on those items that are legally required to be in compliance.

Product title

ProductTitle	
id	ID
product_title	Token
product_version	ProductVersionComplexType

Figure 11: Product title element

This is a complex element which contains the name of the product as assigned by the software manufacturer.

Product version

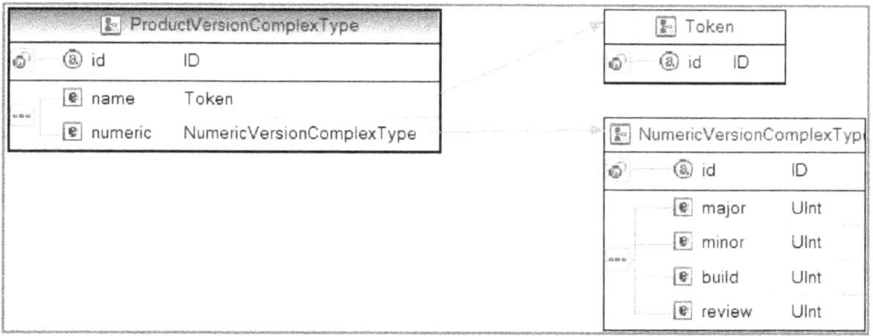

Figure 12: Product version

The version of the product is defined as two elements – numeric version and version name.

This element allows software publishers to provide purely numeric version information which is used for comparison purposes against entitlement information and for grouping purposes. Additionally, the string version is provided so that software manufacturers have the ability to specify any textual representation they want an end-user to see in a report.

Each element is independent, but they should be related and consistent with each other.

The numeric-based version number consists of major and minor version numbers plus build and maintenance numbers. If a publisher/creator does not choose to use all available version numbers, the non-used values should be set to 0. The numeric version can be used for comparison purposes against entitlement information during the reconciliation phase of a SAM process.

The string alternative of the product version may contain numeric and/or alphabetic characters. It is a more user-friendly name of the product version than the numeric-based version number. This value can typically be used in user-oriented reports.

Software creator

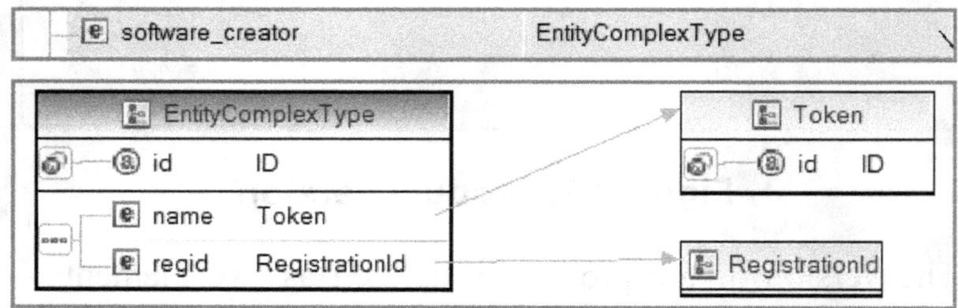

Figure 13: Software creator element

This complex element allows the software management process to identify the specific software manufacturer that created the software package.

Software creator names in different countries may have exactly the same name, but be separate companies. A regid is used to uniquely identify the creator.

Software licensor

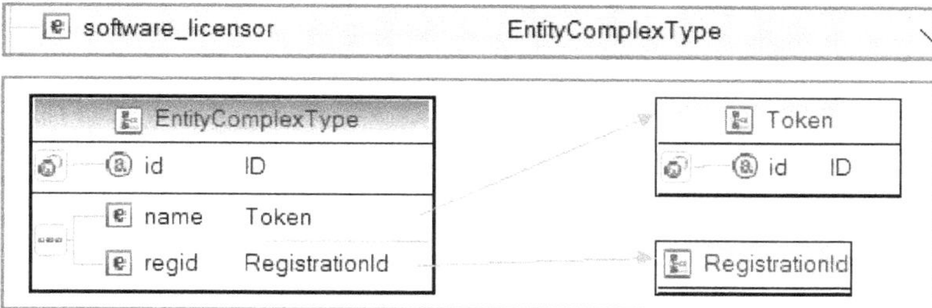

Figure 14: Software licensor element

This complex element identifies the specific software licensor that owns the copyright for the software package. The element contains name and regid as sub-elements.

Software ID

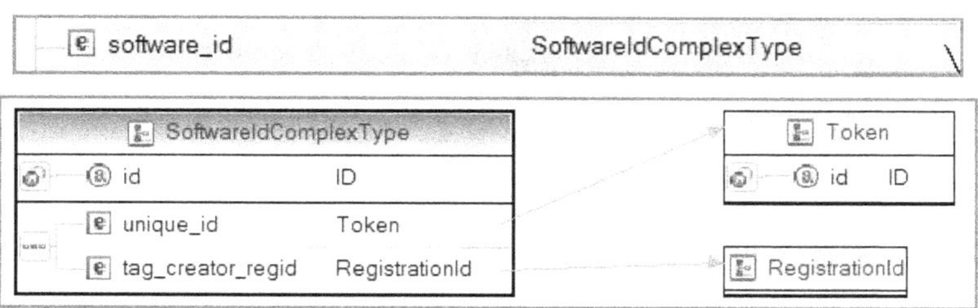

Figure 15: Software ID

The software_id provides information that can be used to reference a specific version of a specific product. It is a requirement that the creator ensures that the unique_id is unique for each software title and version as well as unique to other IDs that may be created by other companies.

Different upgrade levels must be distinguished by unique software identifiers.

Tag creator

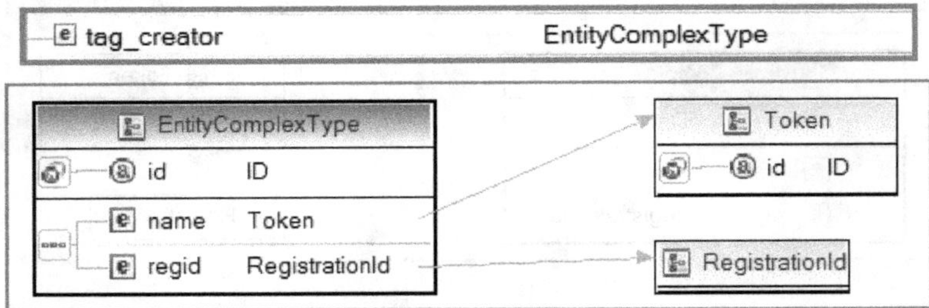

Figure 16: Tag creator attribute

This attribute contains the identity of the tag creator for the component being tagged.

ISO/IEC 19770-2 optional tag elements

Optional identity elements may or may not be provided in a software tag. The content fields that correspond to optional identity elements give software tag creators additional opportunities to improve the reliability of information for software users and tool providers.

Abstract

This is a summary that provides information for the software package that this tag applies to. It includes a language sub-element.

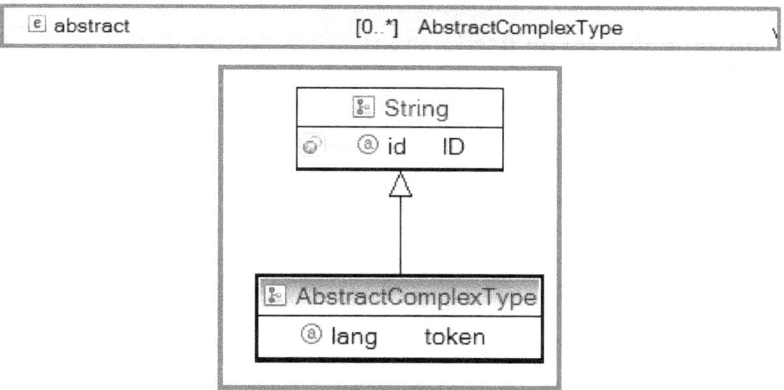

Figure 17: Abstract element

The language element may occur more than once in a software tag, but should only occur once for each language specified. If a language is not specified/present, it should be assumed to be English (en).

Component association

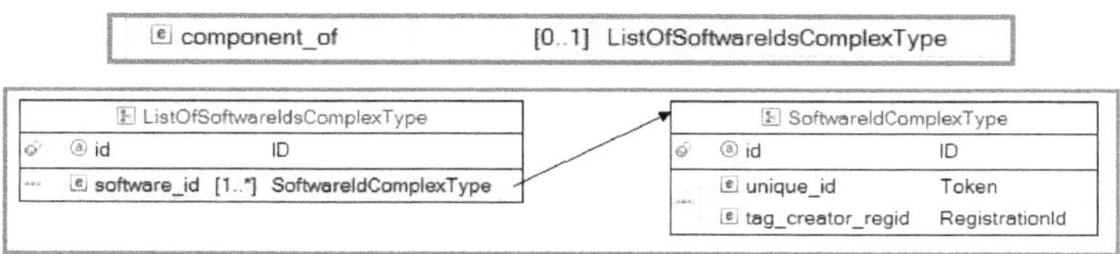

Figure 18: Component of element

This element is used as a mechanism to provide a child-to-parent relationship between packages. Typically, this element can be used when additional components are installed, but are related to an existing package already installed on a computing device.

The element can be used as part of a suite definition as well as in the case where a package is installed which adds functionality to an existing package installed on the computing device.

Components list

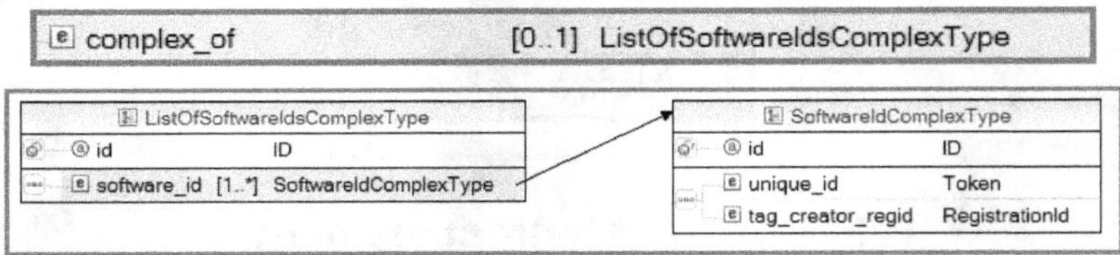

Figure 19: Component list element

This is an element that is used to show parent-to-child relationships (the complement of component_of). This element can provide a list of products that are a part of a suite. The element is made up of a list of unique identifiers that represent the products contained within the suite.

Data source

This element describes the form of media for the original distribution (bag of bits).

Values might be strings such as the following: CD, MSDN CD, Electronic distribution and Definitive software library – Released for distribution.

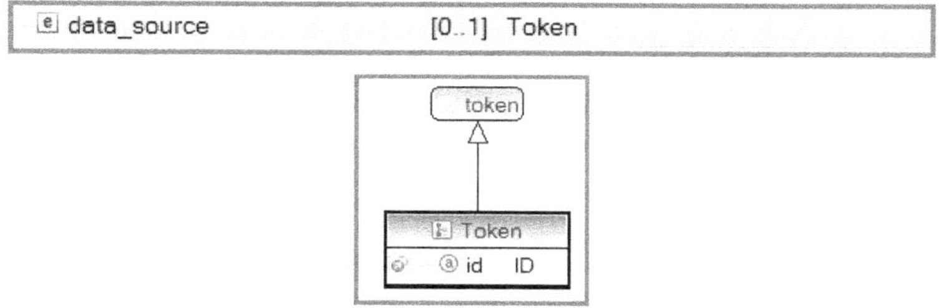

Figure 20: Data source element

Table 2: Data source value definitions

Normalised data value	Definition
physical	The software is being delivered via physical media (CD-ROM, DVD, tape, etc.).
electronic	The installation is coming from a network source. In general, this would indicate that the user is downloading the installation from the Internet.

Dependency

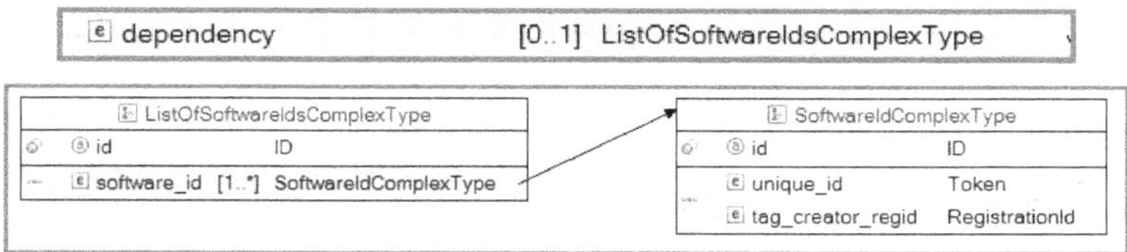

Figure 21: Dependency element

This element is provided to illustrate the dependency of one component upon another in order to run successfully.

For example:

- A Java application is dependent upon a Java VM installation to run properly.
- An Excel® template requires Excel®.

These dependencies are not provided to be used by the software product for configuration validation, but rather to provide guidance to any software life cycle management database with respect to software package/component relationships.

Elements owner

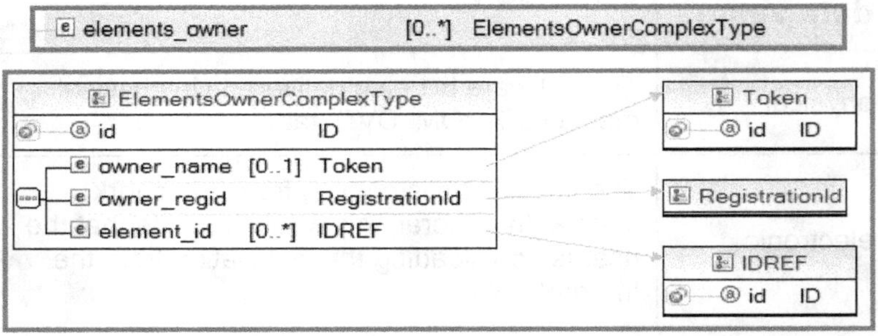

Figure 22: Elements owner

This element provides the ability to specify ownership of elements in the tag. This ownership claim is not as authoritative as using a digital signature; however, it does provide guidance to tag modifiers. By listing an element as being owned, it indicates that the value specified in the element should not be changed unless explicitly agreed to by the existing owner of the element.

The tag creator should specify the elements that may not be modified by any tag modifier. The element utilises element

IDs which the XSD supports. These element IDs are created by the tag creator and need only be uniquely specified and referenced for each software identification tag. The IDs are utilised to reference other specific tag elements from within the tag itself.

Installation details

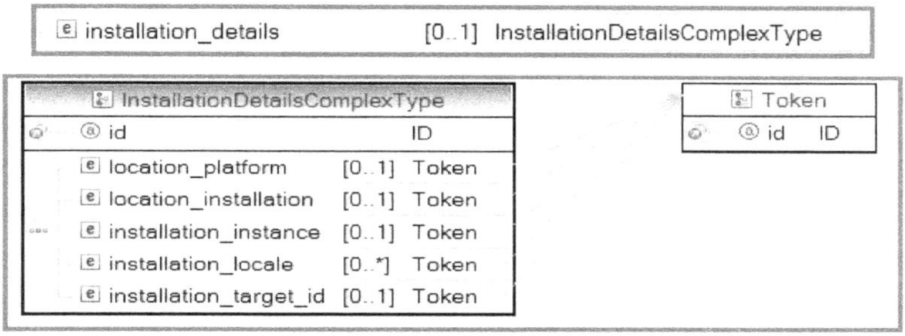

Figure 23: Installation details element

This element provides the full path information on the locations of the software identification tags for a software component installation as well as installation instance details. Each software installation can have two software instances of the same SWID tag added to the system – one in the common platform directory (*see above in ISO/IEC 19770-2 standard tagging locations*), plus one in the root directory of the installed software package.

Installation detail instances are provided for software that is to be installed multiple times on a single platform.

Keywords

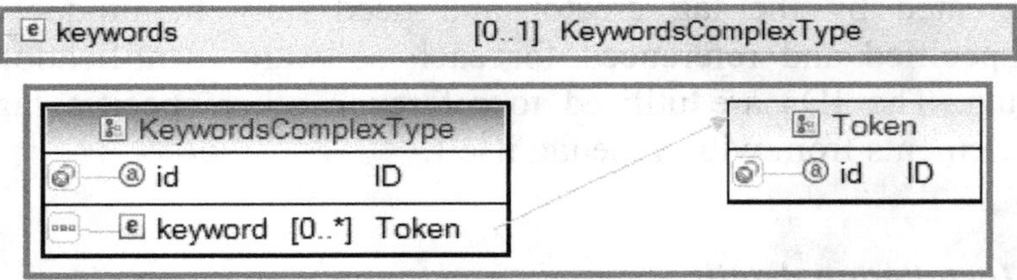

Figure 24: Keywords

A tag creator or modifier may add specific keywords to a SWID tag. The functionality allows for the searching of tags that may be related to specific topics.

Licence linkage

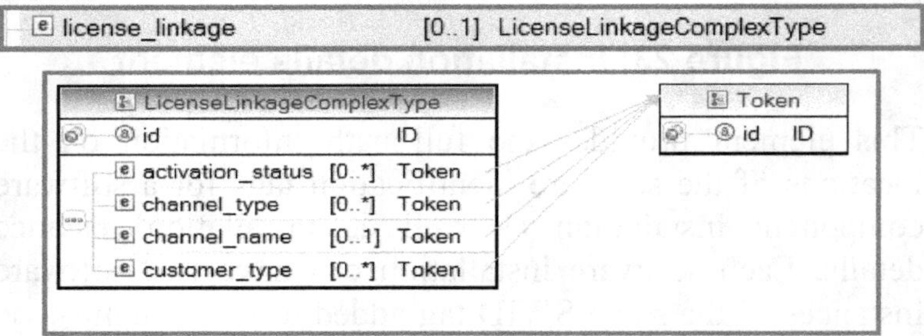

Figure 25: Licence linkage

This element provides licence and channel information and is used as a means to connect an entitlement (or SWEID tag) to this tagged component.

Package footprint

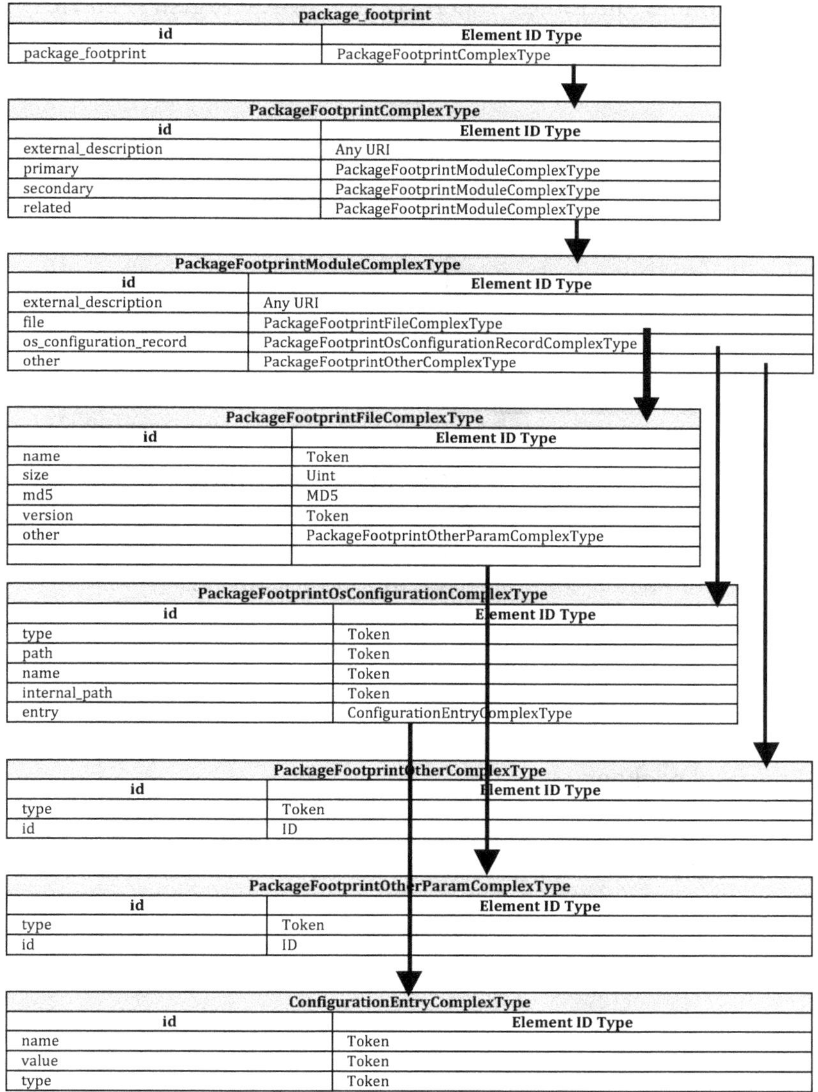

package_footprint	
id	**Element ID Type**
package_footprint	PackageFootprintComplexType

PackageFootprintComplexType	
id	**Element ID Type**
external_description	Any URI
primary	PackageFootprintModuleComplexType
secondary	PackageFootprintModuleComplexType
related	PackageFootprintModuleComplexType

PackageFootprintModuleComplexType	
id	**Element ID Type**
external_description	Any URI
file	PackageFootprintFileComplexType
os_configuration_record	PackageFootprintOsConfigurationRecordComplexType
other	PackageFootprintOtherComplexType

PackageFootprintFileComplexType	
id	**Element ID Type**
name	Token
size	Uint
md5	MD5
version	Token
other	PackageFootprintOtherParamComplexType

PackageFootprintOsConfigurationComplexType	
id	**Element ID Type**
type	Token
path	Token
name	Token
internal_path	Token
entry	ConfigurationEntryComplexType

PackageFootprintOtherComplexType	
id	**Element ID Type**
type	Token
id	ID

PackageFootprintOtherParamComplexType	
id	**Element ID Type**
type	Token
id	ID

ConfigurationEntryComplexType	
id	**Element ID Type**
name	Token
value	Token
type	Token

Figure 26: Package footprint element

This element attempts to specify file sets and other identifiable attributes (such as Windows registry entries) that indicate a product is installed.

Packager

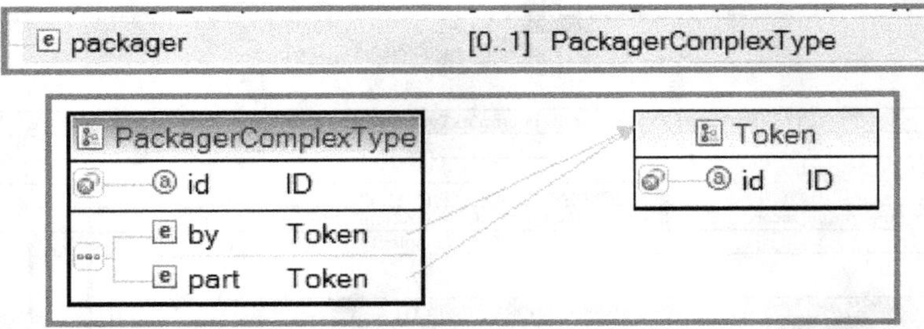

Figure 27: Packager element

The element provides information on modification of the software package for an installation procedure.

This element can be specified by a release manager within an organisation during the process of software configuration of an installation. The packager element can be associated with details such as release_id, and release_package.

The element may also be used by third parties in cases where a product is OEM'd and repackaged.

Product category

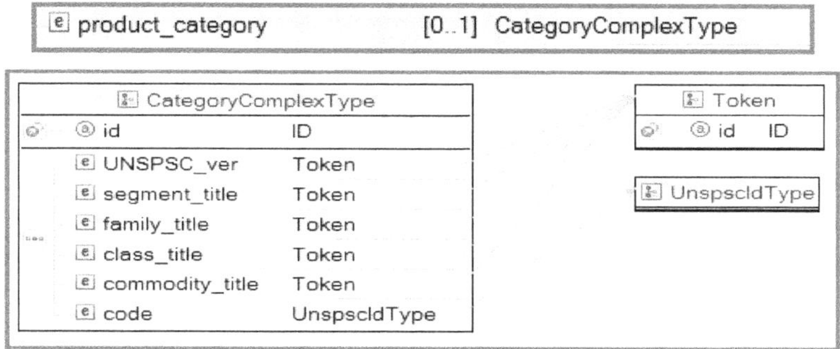

Figure 28: Product category element

This is an element by which product titles can be classified by high-level function using a standardised list. This standard is provided by the United Nations standard products and services code (UNSPSC) (*for more information see www.unspsc.org/*), commodity listing number 43230000. UNSPSC codes are found in the section numbered 43230000 of the specification where the bulk of commonly used software categories can be found.

Product family

product_family	
Id	ID
product_family	string

Figure 29: Product family element

This element provides a method of grouping products together, perhaps for reporting purposes. An example of this might be the case where a product is broken into multiple pieces, a server and a client:

- server application utility – 20 deployments
- client application utility – 10,000 deployed.

Product ID

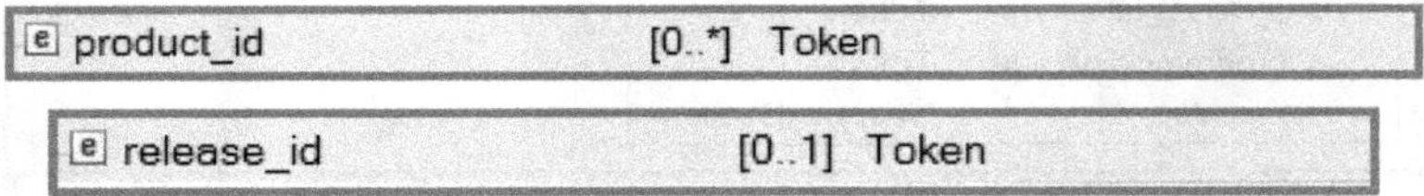

Figure 30: Product ID element

This element is a unique reference across a publisher domain (regid). Symantec has provided the following example:

The product_id for the Application tag is the core product identifier for the application across all product versions even if the application name changes. The standard format of the product_id should be 'iso-pid-<tag_type>-'+ <publisher reference> + '-' + product_title. <tag_type> ::= 'app' | 'cmp' | 'feature' | 'patch' | 'group'. There should be no spaces. Use hyphens in place of spaces. If this release was a new version for a previous release that included tags, then the product_id should be set to the same product_id of the previous release. It is usually the same as the software_id.unique_id where the product_title is the same as the previous release.

For example 'iso-pid-symc-Norton-AntiVirus' would be the same across Norton AntiVirus versions allowing queries to pull all versions of Norton AntiVirus.

Release date

This element is used/updated/modified by a software consumer during the installation/release process. This might include the date the item was released for installation.

release_date	
Id	ID
release_date	DateTime

Figure 31: Release date element

Release ID

release_id	
Id	ID
Release_id	Token

Figure 32: Release ID element

This element is used/updated/modified by a software consumer during the installation/release process. This should be a unique ID across the consumer namespace (regid) and perhaps associated with an entitlement(s) or SWEID.

Release package

This element is used/updated/modified by a software consumer during the installation/release process. The information can be used to verify that the installation/release has been built to conform to specification.

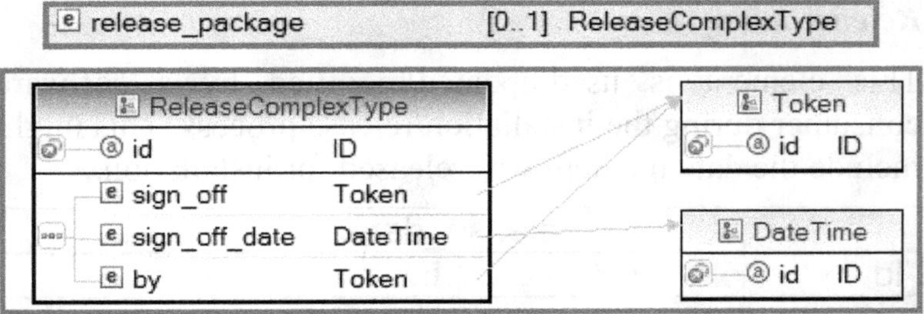

Figure 33: Release package element

Release rollout

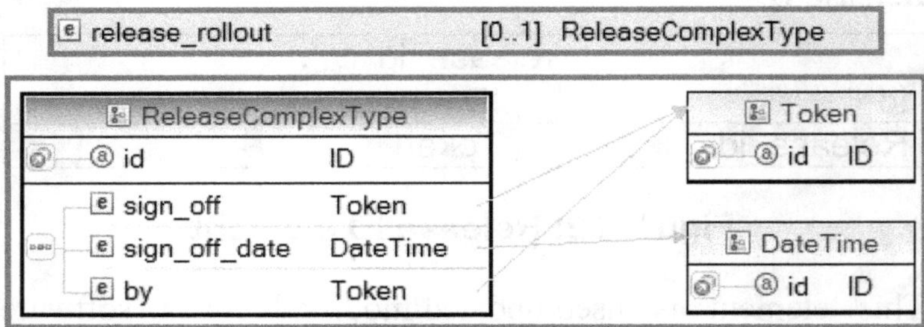

Figure 34: Release rollout element

This element is used/updated/modified by a software consumer during the installation/release process. The information should be the sign-off source and date; it also allows for some free-form information.

Release verification

This element is used/updated/modified by a software consumer during the installation/release process. The information should be the sign-off source and date; it also allows for additional governance information.

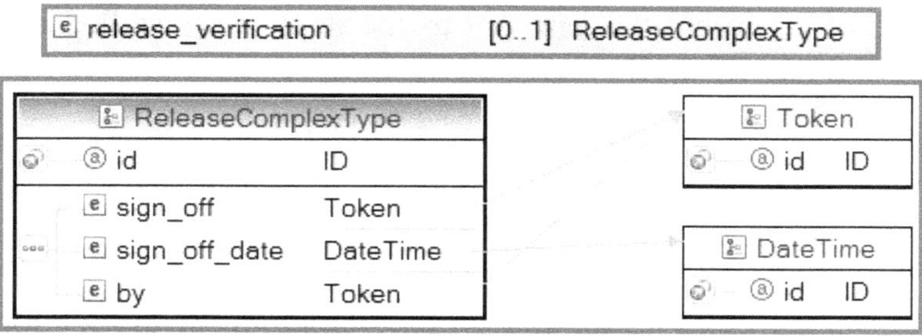

Figure 35: Release verification element

Serial number

Figure 36: Serial number element

This element is very important in the VeriTag software life cycle and may be used to provide a unique identifier within either a publisher namespace (regid) if generated by the publisher in conjunction with generating a uniquely tagged distribution (ESD, etc.), or within the namespace of the consumer if the tag is uniquely generated in the consumer namespace.

The concept of uniquely identified SWID tags is discussed in greater detail later in the sections devoted to creator and consumer tag management.

SKU

Being completely blunt here, I am not sure about what use this is in the -2 tag. When a software product is sold, it is actually an entitlement that is sold and any SKU would be related to an entitlement, not to the deployed/installed bag of bits that a SWID refers to.

Figure 37: SKU element

There is more information on this paradigm in the section addressing tag management for tag creators later.

Software creator

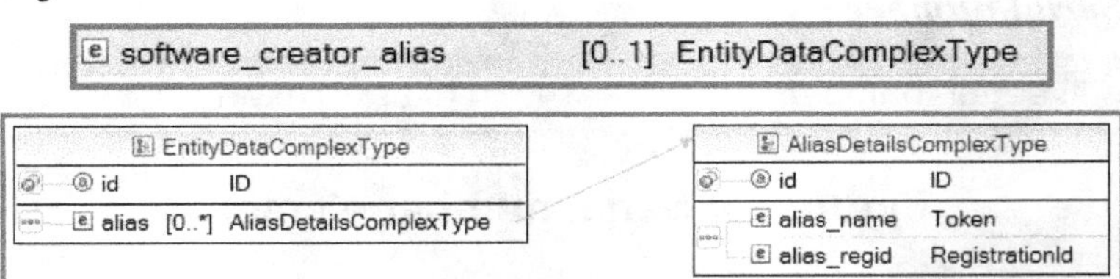

Figure 38: Software creator element

This element contains historical information identifying previous entities which might be related to the software component identified in the tag. Once more, I am not sure of the true value of this information but perhaps it is relevant to SAM processes of which I am not aware.

Software licensor alias

This element is similar in functionality to the software creator element.

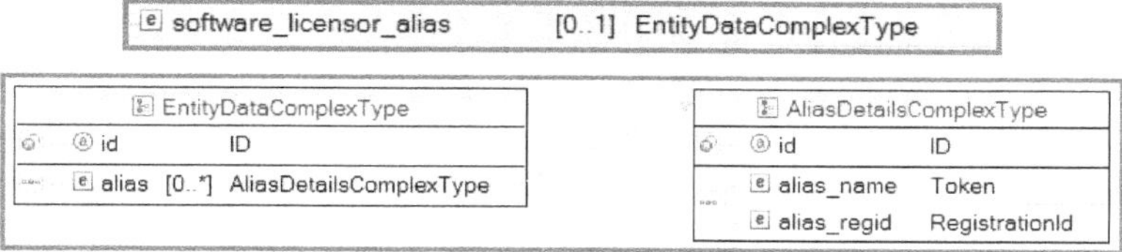

Figure 39: Software licensor element

Supported languages

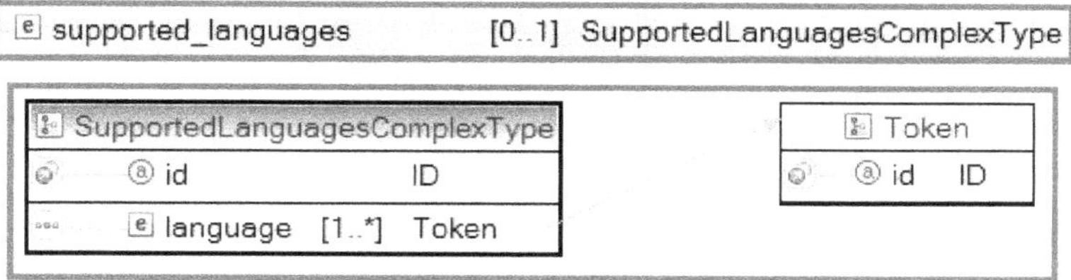

Figure 40: Supported languages element

This element provides the language that the software presents to the user and is specified using the IETF RFC 4646 standard.

Tag creator

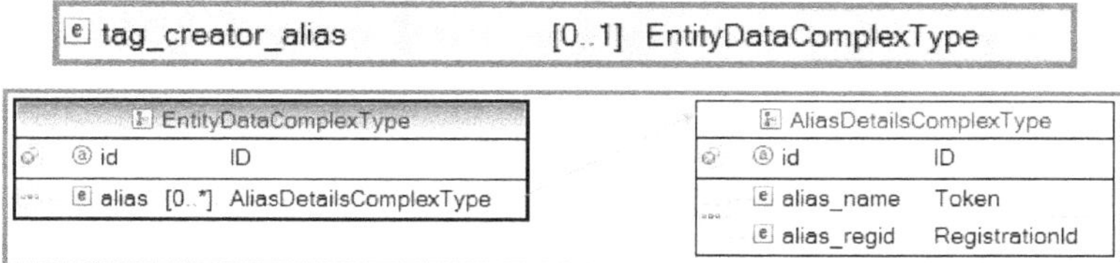

Figure 41: Tag creator element

This element provides additional tag creator information in order to provide identification of previous entities that might be related to the creation of the software tag. This could be used in the scenario where Corporation B has acquired Corporation A and is now publishing software under its own regid. The alias will contain the regid of Corporation A.

Tag creator copyright

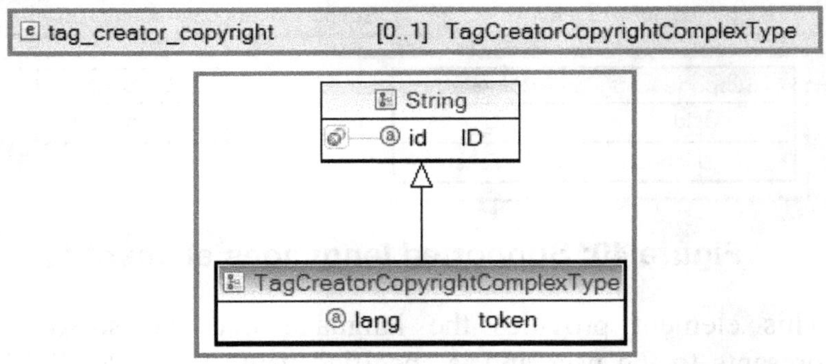

Figure 42: Tag creator copyright element

This element allows for the insertion of a copyright notice covering the content of the tag itself.

Tag version

This is actually an interesting element in that it allows some form of regulation and audit during the tag life cycle (as against the software or entitlement life cycle). There may in fact be multiple instances of this element as the life cycle progresses.

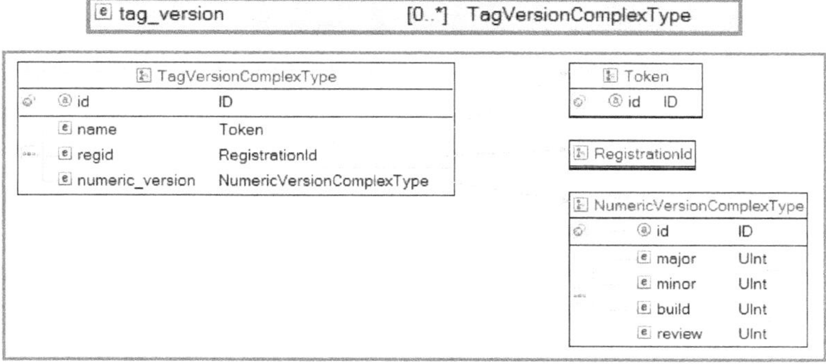

Figure 43: Tag version element

Upgrade for

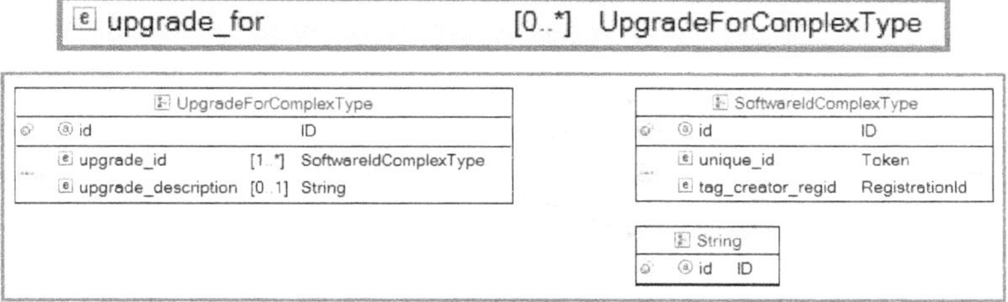

Figure 44: Upgrade element

This element allows upgrade path information to be carried between tags and so allows the update of any management database of accumulated information derived from the tags associated with a particular software product as it evolves.

Usage identifier

The element provides an indication of usage, which according to this standard indicates whether a particular piece of software is executing, which may or may not indicate it is being used.

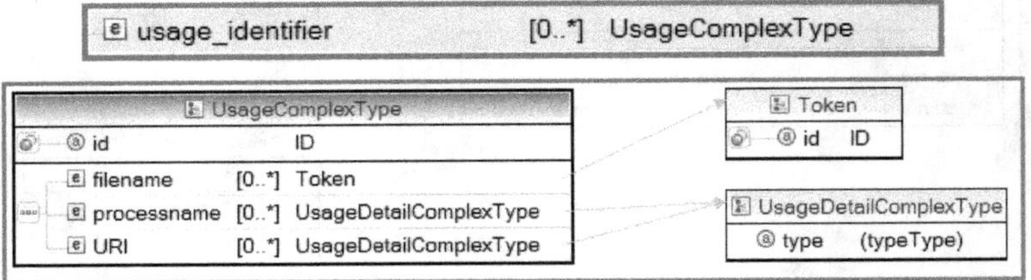

Figure 45: Usage identifier element

True usage can be measured, including metrics and features, in the VeriTag software cycle, and this is described elsewhere in the book.

Validation

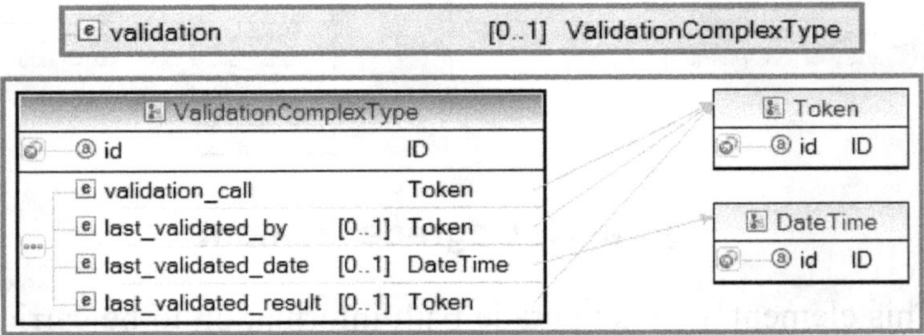

Figure 46: Validation element

This element describes some mechanism, with accompanying date information, which might be used by any function accessing the SWID content that can enable the validation of the tag. The function could exist within the software that is itself tagged, or some other external mechanism.

ISO/IEC 19770-2 extended identity elements

Extended information is provided in the software tag to allow the inclusion of additional values that have not been predefined. Extended information must be in an XML format and should include an XSD reference that can be used to validate the information in this section.

Unlike the mandatory and optional sections, there may be multiple extended sections in a tag. Each extended section can be available for only one specific owner. For example, a software publisher may include extended information that they want included for their own discovery tool. An end-user organisation may want to include extended information related to their overall software life cycle policies and procedures.

Extended information

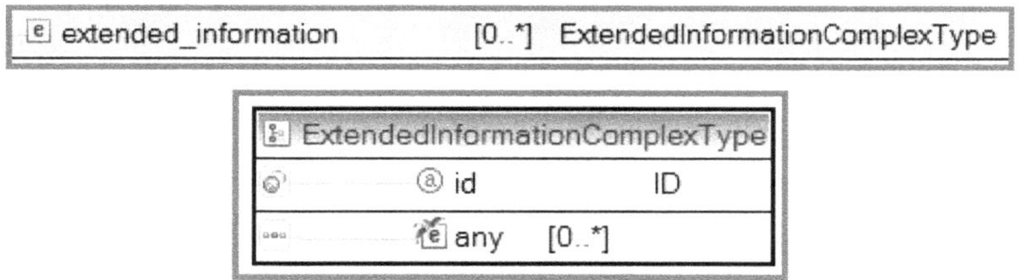

Figure 47: Extended information element

The sub-elements may be provided by the creator, modifier or consumer. There should be an XSD available, and referred to, which describes any element.

CHAPTER 7: SWID TAG CERTIFICATION REQUIREMENTS

TagVault.org

In the US, the current body offering regulation and assistance in tagging standards is TagVault.org. The stated mission is as follows:

TagVault.org is the neutral not-for-profit certification authority for software tagging, primarily focused on software identification tags (as specified by ISO/IEC 19770-2) and software entitlement tags (as specified by ISO/IEC 19770-3). By providing a trusted certification process for software identification and software entitlement definitions to software publishers, tool providers, and end-users, the expensive and complicated issue of software asset governance/compliance will be greatly simplified.

TagVault.org will:

1 Certify software products and software publishers that provide 19770-2, 19770-3 or other software identification tags, tools that utilize these tags and operating systems that provide management facilities for software identification.
2 Provide certification marks to member organizations in good standing for use in their marketing literature and packaging.
3 Promote the Members of the Organization as well as the benefits of certified products to the general market place.
4 Advance the adoption, use and evolution of interoperable, internationally accepted standards, specifications and guidelines for a certifiable process of reconciliation for software assets.
5 Enable organizations and individuals from the software industry, enterprise users of licensed software, and service providers attendant to the software and software services supply chain to collaborate globally on development and sharing of central, standardized infrastructure for software tags using a process that is open, democratic and sustainable.

6 Support users of standardized software tagging tools and technology by providing or sponsoring SAM-tagging related standards, service publications, professional events and technology development.

I recommend membership at one of the various levels if you are at all interested in this topic (and if you have read this far into the book, you surely must be!). Despite its US origins, the organisation is reaching a worldwide audience and is a global source of information and assistance.

Overview of certification

Any tag that is submitted to be a certified tag must minimally meet the requirements of base certification (*see below*). Additionally, if the certified tag is designated to receive a higher level of certification, it must also meet all additional requirements specified by the level of certification desired.

Note: all elements that have normalised data values specified in data normalisation must utilise data values as specified or must register new data values, which can be accomplished as specified in the same section below.

US Federal Government draft GSA/DoD requirement

The proposed draft language for use in government contracts for implementing software ID and entitlement tagging is as follows:

Quoted from Draft Tag Clause for SmartBUY (7/28/2010)

Software Tagging: Unless modified by delivery order, commercial-off-the-shelf software products released for production after January 1, 2011 shall include a software identification tag that conforms to the International Standard for

Software Identification Tagging, ISO/IEC 19770-2:2009. The minimum level for software identification tags required by this procurement is to provide the specified mandatory elements as designated by ISO/IEC 19770-2:2009 and provide optional elements as may be designated by the delivery order.

Certification levels

Multiple certification levels are available for SWID tags. As part of the certification process, TagVault.org has extended the ISO/IEC 19770-2:2009 XSD schema to include:

- name of the certification authority
- certificate authority reference information
- unique registration identifier
- certification level applied to this specific SWID tag.

These extensions have been done in a manner that conforms to the ISO/IEC 19770-2:2009 standard. (Refer to the requirements of ISO/IEC 19770-2:2009 as listed below.)

These values are only be applied by the certification authority and are added to the SWID tag as part of the certification process. The data elements for these items are shown in the structure below. The XML element must be signed by the certification authority when the tag is certified.

Base certification requirements

Summary

Base certification is the initial level of certification for SWID tags. This level of certification requires the seven mandatory elements specified by the ISO/IEC 19770-

2:2009 standard to be included in the tag. This level of certification provides SAM and other software life cycle management practitioners with specific provenance details on who the publisher is, which product is installed and a unique ID that can be utilised to access more information about the product from the TagVault.org repository or from the publisher. (The VTP internal repository contains all publisher SWID tag information, if used to create and manage SWID tags for the publisher. When the TagVault.org repository becomes available, VTP can optionally allow the publisher to update the TagVault.org repository either manually or automatically, as required.)

If additional data elements are included in this tag, they can be validated to ensure they conform to the specifications described in this document. However, to receive a base certification, additional data elements are not required to be included in the tag. Also, additional elements can not be digitally signed by TagVault.org. (If the publisher is using VTP to create and manage SWID tags, they may, optionally, be digitally signed if desired.)

XML validation requirements

When a software ID tag is submitted to TagVault.org for certification, that tag goes through the following validation steps.

Conformance validation requirements

- Is the externally defined XSD available via the specified uniform resource identifier (URI) reference?

- Is the XML document a valid document (i.e. it is well formed and conforms to the constraints of the ISO XSD and any externally defined XSD)?
- Do the contents of the XML document conform to the ISO/IEC 19770-2:2009 standard – specifically, to clause 2.2.3?

Required data elements

TagVault.org certification validation requirements

- Is the publisher a current registered member of TagVault.org or has the publisher paid for a single certification process?
- Was the tag delivered from a registered user who works for the publisher (tags may only be provided by those individuals who have been authorised by the company to create certified tags)?
- Has a core regid been registered?
- Is the regid a tag-ready regid (i.e. it includes a suffix)?
- Does the tag pass all conformance requirements?
- Do data values utilised in the elements use the normalised data values defined by TagVault.org members?
- Is the unique ID unique within the scope of the tag_creator_regid?

If the tag is found to conform to the specification and to TagVault.org certification requirements, the seven mandatory elements are digitally signed by TagVault.org with a VeriSign code signing certificate. Once signed, the certified tag is checked into the TagVault.org repository and provided back to the publisher.

(If the tag creator is using VTP to create and manage SWID tags, these requirements can be met and verified automatically (including the TagVault.org SWID signing and check-in service) via built-in web service interfaces with TagVault.org.)

Asset management certification

Summary

Asset management certification builds on the base certification. All requirements specified for base certification must be achieved in addition to the requirements specified for asset management certification.

This level of certification requires additional data elements in a SWID tag that are useful for the SAM practitioner to have available. This level of certification can often be specified as a requirement for GSA/DoD COTS software purchases in request for information (RFI) and request for proposal (RFP) documents. Software that achieves this level of certification is much easier to manage as an asset because the additional data provided allows more in-depth analysis and the data can help SAM practitioners manage by exception. (Management by exception means that organisations have enough reliable data from the software discovery process such that policies and rules may be defined, requiring SAM practitioners' specialised attention only when discovered software does not match the specified policy or rules.)

Required elements

On top of the seven mandatory elements specified in the ISO/IEC 19770-2:2009 standard, the additional elements required to achieve asset management certification are outlined below.

Table 3: Required elements

Element name	Signed at certification	Restriction
Abstract	No	Maximum of 4096 bytes of data for the textual component of the element
Component_of	Yes	Tags related to one another must either be submitted at the same time, or TagVault.org must have already certified referenced tags
Complex_of	Yes	Tags related to one another must either be submitted at the same time, or TagVault.org must have already certified referenced tags
Package_footprint	Yes, but only the details for the primary file entries	At least one entry must be provided in the primary definition of package_footprint

Product_category	Yes	All product category references must match details provided in the UNSPSC version specified
Product_id	No	Flexible

Desired elements

The items in Table 4 are also desired elements in a SWID tag. However, these may be generated dynamically (and therefore are not signed).

Table 4: Desired elements

Element name	Signed at certification	Description
Installation_locale	No	The installation_locale element that is found in the installation_details element grouping provides details about which locale or locales are supported by a particular software product for the installation on a specific computing device. The locales are specified by IETF RFC 4646 as the region (page 11 of the IETF RFC 4646 document).

Activation_status	No	The activation_status element located in the license_linkage element group provides specific details on the current activation state of the software product referred to by the SWID tag. Activation as specified in this document refers to specific states a software product may be in and is advisory in nature and not intended to provide proof that a product is in a particular state.
Channel_type	No	The channel_type element located in the license_linkage element group provides specific details on which channel the installed software is intended for. This element can almost always be added to the tag at installation time and can be based on installation characteristics (often based on the product code entered).
Customer_type	No	Similar to the channel_type element, the customer_type element located in the license_linkage element group provides specific

		details on which customer type the installed software is intended for. This element can almost always be added to the tag at installation time and can be based on installation characteristics (often based on the product code entered).
Product_family	No	This element allows SAM practitioners to group together software items that may not be purchased together, but may be related – such as client and server components, or back-up software.
Product_id	No	This element provides an identifier that may be used to identify product lineage as products are upgraded.

TagVault.org normalisation

Regid

As a result of initial work carried out with Symantec, one of the base elements, regid (complex type), has been extended to allow for large corporation business practices.

TagVault.org strengthens the definition of regid provided by the ISO/IEC 19770-2 standard. The standard defined regids without the expectation that a registration authority would be available, which offered easier industry adoption but did not provide the level of structure required to ensure consistency. With TagVault.org acting as a registration authority, the regid definition can be strengthened to mandate consistency without adversely affecting industry adoption of the standard.

Let's look at an example regid. We can use Symantec as our example organisation.

A regid consists of:

- the string 'regid'
- a period (.) separator
- the date at which the entity creating the regid first owned the domain that is also used in the regid in year-month format YYYY-MM, e.g. 1992-12 (MM is the first month the owner owned the domain on the first day of the month at 00:01 GMT)
- a period (.) separator
- the domain of the entity, in reverse order: 'com.symantec'
- a comma (,)
- an optional suffix.

Symantec's base regid is therefore: regid.1992-12.com.symantec.

The standard allows for, but does not require, additional sub-entities that are added as a suffix to the above regid. These may appear as follows:

- regid.1992-12.com.symantec,Altiris

- regid.1992-12.com.symantec,Norton.

TagVault.org's certified regids require that at least one suffix is used. TagVault.org's regid rules are shown in Table 5.

Table 5: Regid rules

Certified base regid (Cannot be used in any SWID tag)	regid.1992-12.com.symantec
Certified sub-entity regid (may be used in any SWID tag)	regid.1992-12.com.symantec, Altiris
Certified sub-entity regid (may be used in any SWID tag)	regid.1992-12.com.symantec, Norton

By requiring that a certified sub-entity regid is also created for use, TagVault.org ensures that SAM and other software life cycle management practitioners can easily roll up or group all SWID tags according to the primary licensing organisation.

This structure provides a benefit to the software publisher as well. By creating a certified regid for each development group, each group can develop and release its products independently of a centralised release manager. Note that the use of multiple sub-entities is not required. If a software publisher prefers to use a single regid for publication, it may do this by registering a base regid and a single sub-entity regid which it then uses for all SWID tags.

Name

Each element that includes a regid also includes a name. It's not defined as a requirement in the ISO/IEC 19770-2:2009 standard that the name remains consistent (the standard indicates that the name 'should be consistent between software products and software releases'). However, TagVault.org certified tags can ensure that every TagVault.org registered regid includes a specified name and that the name matches the name specified in the registration. Spaces can be trimmed from the front and back of the string and ignored.

Software_id.unique_id

This element is a string and does not have a specific structure defined – it's free-form for the software publisher. This element must, however, follow restrictions for URI references as specified in IETF RFC 3986, Section 2. Additionally, the unique_id must not have any characters that are inconsistent with filenames on any platform the software can be installed on – these include /, \, [, etc. Unique_id must be unique for the specified tag_creator_regid.

Data_source

This element specifies where the original source of the installation came from. If this element is provided, it can provide information to a SAM and other software life cycle management practitioners as to what media the installation came from. Note that the data_source element is likely to increase in size and options as various publishers specify their own media structures for software delivery.

Keywords

This element is intended to be flexible and applied by the software development team. Keywords provide a publisher as well as software customers with the ability to create a keyword cloud to describe the software identified by this SWID tag. This element was created to help SAM practitioners get a general feeling for the software installations of a particular group using free-form tag keywords.

There are, however, constraints in the TagVault.org certification. The ISO/IEC 19770-2:2009 standard allows any number of data values to be supplied for the keyword element and does not put a restriction on the length of the data values. TagVault.org certification requirements put more restrictions on this to make it more practical to use in a production environment. TagVault.org certification requirement restrictions include the following:

- Each keyword data value shall be 40 characters or fewer – enabling discovery, inventory, SAM and other software life cycle management tools to provide ready access to keyword data values through list operations (selection or drop-down lists).
- A SWID tag shall not include more than 25 publisher-defined keyword data values – imposing practical limits on the number of data values applied to any one keyword element for a given software product from a single publisher minimises the negative impact of 'cloud mapping' of keyword data values simply for a potential marketing opportunity on the part of publishers, with little to no benefit to the SAM practitioner and unnecessary requirements for discovery/inventory tool vendors.

- No duplicate data values are allowed within a single software tag – this also minimises the negative impacts to SAM practitioners and discovery/inventory tool vendors of repetitive keyword data values.

Activation_status

This element provides details on how complete a software installation is. TagVault.org certified tags must be populated with one of the values in Table 6.

Table 6: Activation status values

Normalised data value	Definition
trial	The product is in a trial mode of operation, typically for evaluation purposes.
pre-release	The product identified by this SWID tag is a pre-release product and, in general, can require specialised entitlements and can generally not be expected to be used in any production environment. This can often refer to alpha and beta releases of a software product.
unlicensed	The product identified by this SWID tag has been installed, but may not have been executed or may not have been able to connect to a website to authenticate that the end-user has rights to install and use the product.
activated	The product identified by this SWID tag is available for the end-user to use in a production environment.

Channel_type

The channel_type is intended to provide details of which channel the product is delivered through. This allows a publisher to track software that's targeted for one channel and may show up in a different channel market. For example, if software targeted for an academic or government channel is showing up in as enterprise, it could be an indication that the software did not follow the expected distribution channel properly. If this element is included in a TagVault.org certified tag, it must be populated with one of the values in Table 7.

Table 7: Channel type values

Normalised data value	Definition
academic	Targeted at the educational market.
government	Targeted at the government market.
OEM	OEM versions are often installed on systems as they are purchased and often have additional restrictions on them (such as limited or no transfer rights).
reseller	Targeted at the reseller or VAR market.
retail	Targeted at retail, or over-the-counter type sales channels.
training	Targeted at training organisations, or for enterprise training locations.
volume	Targeted at enterprise volume installations. Larger enterprises can utilise volume licences

	to lower licensing costs as well as to allow for easier installation and updates (often volume licensed products do not have the same installation requirements that require the end-user at the computer to input a licensing key). For this type of enterprise, if products targeted for a retail channel are installed, it raises an exception with the SAM practitioner to identify why.

Channel_name

This element is a string element that specifies a reseller or partner name. There are no specific values that must be used in this element to conform to TagVault.org certification requirements.

This value may be used for support or renewal purposes and is provided to allow the software purchaser to identify exactly which vendor the media used to install the software was delivered from.

Customer_type

The customer_type is similar to, but slightly different from, channel_type. Channel_type defines the distribution channel a software product is expected to follow. For example, it is possible that a software product is distributed through a retail channel, but is intended to be utilised by academic customers. Customer_type defines the type of customer that is expected to install the software. If this element is included in TagVault.org certified tags, it must be populated with one of the normalised data values in Table 8.

Table 8: Customer type values

Normalised data value	Definition
academic	Targeted at the educational market.
enterprise	Targeted at larger commercial businesses.
demo	Targeted at users who provide demonstrations of a software product. Demo versions are typically not meant to be installed in production environments.
development	Targeted at the software development community to be used for application development and test only – not for production use.
government	Targeted at the government market.
non-profit	Targeted at non-profit organisations.
OEM	OEM versions are often installed on systems as they are purchased and often have additional restrictions on them (such as limited or no transfer rights).
personal	Targeted for personal or home use only.
reseller	Targeted at the reseller or VAR market.
retail	Targeted at retail, or over-the-counter type sales channels.
training	Targeted at training organisations, or for enterprise training locations.

volume	Targeted at enterprise volume installations. In general, volume installations can have fewer issues with product keys and installation restrictions.

Package_footprint

For the base and asset management levels of certification, primary_elements, a sub-element of package_footprint, can be used by discovery tools to provide a relationship between SWID tags and application recognition libraries. This allows discovery tools to quickly and authoritatively identify that a discovered executable file (which is often used to identify software) is related to a discovered SWID tag.

Package_footprint provides a structure that software publishers can use to specify primary, secondary and related files, and other system configurations that are part of a software product installation. When the standard was written, the MD5 algorithm was defined as the cryptographic hash algorithm to use to identify a file. In general, the MD5 hash algorithm provides sufficiently secure identification of files. However, additional security may be desired by software publishers or their customers.

For each file specified in the package_footprint data structure, an 'other' entry is allowed. This entry includes a name and value. This 'other' data structure was designed to allow data, in addition to that published in the ISO/IEC 19770-2:2009 standard, to be included with a file and is the appropriate location for supporting other hash algorithms.

Note: in the initial definition of certified tags, the determination to use the MD5 or secure hash algorithm

(SHA) digests (or both) is left to the software manufacturer. In future levels of certification, it is expected that the requirements could specify that SHA-2 digests be used.

Tag_creator_copyright

This element is not a strict requirement for certification, but should be included if possible. VTE (and potentially other SWID harvesting tools) collects software ID tags and stores them in systems separate from the software. If a software publisher has a policy that a software tag may not be stored, copied and transferred independently of the software title, the utilisation of that software tag diminishes significantly. By explicitly providing a copyright statement such as the following, discovery tools, and third-party tag aggregators are able to function efficiently without having any negative impact on the software publisher's revenue streams or IP rights.

TagVault.org's suggested copyright statement:

Copyright <year> by <company>, all rights reserved. This XML document may be accessed, stored, copied and transferred by any software tool provider or third-party tag collection/distribution agency as long as the following elements are not modified:

- entitlement_required_indicator
- product_title
- product_version
- software_creator
- software_licensor
- software_id
- tag_creator.

Extended information may also be added to the tag.

Additional validation by Symantec Corporation

For those interested in co-operating with Symantec Corporation, the following proposals for normalisation have been submitted, and will be included in SWID tags created by Symantec Corporation:

- **product_title** – used as a display name in reports. It should be normalised with the marketing name for the item that the tag corresponds to. For example, if the tag is an application tag, then the product_title should be consistent with how the application or product is referenced on entitlement records, marketing/pricing documents, etc. but should not include version information. This will allow reports to be grouped based on the name across versions. Tools can group based product_title and product_version.name to get a breakdown of titles by version, e.g. Symantec BackupExec, Symantec Endpoint Protection.
- **product_version** – two sub-elements, name and numeric:
    - Name is the string name or marketing name for the version. For example, '2010' in the case of BackupExec 2010, or '7.0' for NetBackup 7.0.
    - Numeric is the numeric form of the version – major.minor.build.revision, e.g. 9.0.103.1.
- **software_id** – this is the unique ID for the application version and unique for the tag:
    - tag_creator_regid – the same regid as specified in the software_licensor element
    - unique_id – 'iso-sid-<tag_type>-' + <publisher reference> + '-' + product_title + '-' + product_version.name. <tag_type> ::= 'app' | 'cmp' | 'feature' | 'patch' | 'group'. It should not have any

spaces. Use hyphens in place of spaces. Having a standard element format within the associated tag makes it easy to visually correlate the software_id with the company (e.g. element = 'iso-sid-cmp-symc-BackupExec-Server-2010') and the application (e.g. element = 'iso-sid-app-symc-BackupExec-2010').

- **product_id** – the product_id for the application tag is the core product identifier for the application across all product versions, even if the application name changes. The standard format of the product_id should be 'iso-pid-<tag_type>-'+ <publisher reference> + '-' + product_title. <tag_type> ::= 'app' | 'cmp' | 'feature' | 'patch' | 'group'. It should not have any spaces. Use hyphens in place of spaces. If this release was a new version for a previous release that included tags, then the product_id should be set to the same product_id of the previous release. It is usually the same as the software_id.unique_id where the product_title is the same as the previous release, e.g. 'iso-pid-symc-Norton-AntiVirus', so would be the same across Norton AntiVirus versions, allowing queries to pull all versions of Norton AntiVirus.
- **tag_type** – this is a custom element that indicates the type of -2 tag – application, patch, etc. This field is set to 'Application', 'Patch', 'Group', 'Feature' or 'Component'.

CHAPTER 8: ISO/IEC 19770-3 CONSIDERATIONS

Proposed ISO/IEC 19770-3 software entitlement ID tag functionality

ISO/IEC 19770-3 will provide a standard to specify the structure of software entitlement tags. Software entitlement ID tags are XML data structures that provide authoritative identifying information about software licensing rights. In 'Candide's ideal world', the degree of an organisation's software licence compliance configurations will be demonstrated when 19770-3 entitlement tags are reconciled with 19770-2 SWID tags.

If you detected some of Voltaire's satirical edge in my statement above, you will not be surprised, given my earlier description of the fuzzy rules when interpreting the information delivered by SWID tags.

The dream of automating reconciliation is still difficult to achieve using the two kinds of tag in any but the simplest of licensing scenarios. However, what the SWEID does bring to the table is a standard way of expressing entitlement such that it allows a supplier of entitlements to deliver the information in a clear fashion and in a manner that is machine readable.

Overview of the SWEID tag

Much like the SWID tag, the SWEID tag is an encapsulation of rights and limitations, as well as the appropriate metrics, for an entitlement in an XML format.

As can be seen from our life cycle diagram (*see Figure 4*), the entitlement is created as a result of an agreement between licensee and licensor as to which aspects of a predefined licence are entitled.

The predefined licence is instantiated in the very first step of our cycle when the product manager is designing the offerings, that is to say features and meters. There is more detail on this process later. The entitlement is generated and delivered in the 'Deliver Software &/or Service Client' step as the result of some transaction that entitles the licensor to some aspect of these features and metrics.

The entitlement information may be used by both licensor and licensee throughout the remaining life cycle during reconciliations, true-ups, renewals and updates, as required.

Identifying a SWEID tag

Tags *should* be created with IDs but this is not required by the standard. There are some commercial models in which the publisher must create tags ahead of time because control the distribution is not required. Additionally, the entitled functionality does not have any post-acquisition processes such as registration or activation. Examples might be as follows:

- Perpetual products: they are picked up at a store where the software package has no follow-on entitlement (renewal, upgrade, etc.). Restriction in deployment/usage is usually hard-enforced within the product and requires no follow-up process on the part of the licensor.
- Demo: this is a software package handed out at a trade show on DVDs without registration. Again, restriction in deployment/usage is usually hard-enforced within the

product and requires no follow-up process on the part of the licensor.

- Freeware/Shareware: these are software packages which are given away for free (shareware or freeware licensing models).
- Trial: similar to the demo scenario above, the software package can be downloaded with an 'X-day' use from any number of websites prior to being purchased. As above, restriction in deployment/usage is usually hard-enforced within the product and requires no follow-up process on the part of the licensor.

A common aspect of all of these scenarios is that the licensor is an anonymous consumer, thus requiring no identification of either themselves or their asset as far as the licensor/service consumer is concerned. Mere possession of the product, which itself contains any entitlement information (hopefully tamper-proofed in some fashion), qualifies as being in compliance with any licence agreement.

The mechanism by which this agreement is reached has been the subject of many debates, but is not considered here.

There are several reasons why a licensor may wish to issue tags in these scenarios:

- To help licensors/service consumers differentiate between store-bought software and volume program pricing. This is often reported as a large reconciliation issue – especially for low-priced items.
- To reassure consumers (and software life cycle management tools) that there are no restrictions or

limitations of use. For example, a freeware program might limit use to non-commercial work.

- To differentiate between the rights of a time-limited entitlement (downloaded from any site) and those of a fully entitled software package.

If a SWEID tag does have an ID, this ID must be unique across the tag ID namespace of the tag creator. The ID should be indexed in some fashion to the business transaction (enabling the 'Deliver Software &/or Service Client' step in our life cycle) generating it, otherwise understanding the tag's business relevance is impossible.

SWEID tag modification or replacement

SWEID tag creators may require an entitlement to be updated. Scenarios might include the following:

- Consumer converts a standard to a premium version of the software package.
- Consumer upgrades from version 1 to version 2.
- Consumer adds additional capacity to an existing software package (goes from 10 users to 50 users).
- Consumer adds a feature to an existing software package (connector to a different type of hardware or support for another RDBMS).
- Consumer converts from a trial to a full version.
- Consumer gets purchased by another company and all their entitlements are transferred to the new entity.

The -3 proposed standard has two approaches to this:

1 Publisher can issue a -3 tag with the same tag_id (implying an update). This is called the replacement approach.
2 Publishers can issue a new -3 tag with a new tag_id and (if appropriate) a -3 tag removing the previous -3 tag tag_id. This is called the add/archive, cumulative or atomic approach.

From experience, the second approach is easier to implement for both the creator and consumer, plus it is much easier to manage since there is a built-in audit trail in the process.

The proposed standard currently says the software publishers could implement the second approach and then change to the first approach. The proposed standard also currently says software publishers could use both methods – depending on the transaction type.

Again, experience says that changing any licensing or entitlement paradigm during the life cycle of a product causes unimaginable management problems for both the creator and consumer.

Children SWEID tags

In some scenarios, consumers may wish to add information to SWEID tags. For example, a consumer might add a purchase order number (or the consumer-side index) to the entitlement-generating business transaction. This can be achieved by adding the information and signing the original tag. These are not children tags.

Consumers, however, may wish to modify/change the information provided in the original tag. Examples of scenarios might be:

- A multinational purchases a large quantity to receive some large discount. The multinational then wishes to split those entitlements across multiple countries to provide local organisations with control of their own quantities. These local countries might then split those quantities further for different locations.
- A university purchases large quantities from a publisher and then wants to allocate them across multiple departments.

These new tags are called children tags. Children tags can be created by consumers. Children tags have the following characteristics:

- They have their own unique tag_id. This will, of course, be the responsibility of the child tag creator to ensure.
- Linkage to their parents will be achieved by recording the original tag (root_id) and the immediate parent (parent_id). By following this structure, children tags can have grandchildren tags and great-great-great grandchildren tags and this lineage can be traced to the first – root – tag.
- Children tags may include any and/or all parts of the original publisher tag into the child.
- Children tags may create children of children of children… as much as they want.
- Children tags may override/augment any of the attributes of the original tag. For example, they could provide a new quantity and a new user entity.

Creators of children SWEID tags have a number of responsibilities:

- Creators of children SWEID tags should prevent a user from over-creating or over-splitting quantities. For example – if an original tag has 1,000 seats, then a child tag creator should prevent a user from creating a child tag with 1,500 seats. Creators of children SWEID tags should also track the splitting so that if the user creates 800 for department A, they should prevent the user from creating 500 for department B. The VTE tool incorporates this functionality into child SWEID creation automatically.
- Creators of children SWEID tags should prevent a user from overriding publisher-only data such as metrics. Again, the VTE tool incorporates this functionality into child SWEID creation automatically.

SWEID tag types

As previously mentioned, SWEID tags are intended to keep track of more than software entitlements. The goal is to assist publishers and customers to track any right to use, as well as any right to service or right to access as might be the case for SaaS functions or content management.

The proposed standard contains some fundamental archetypes for entitlements:

- Licence: this implies the right to use a particular software package. This right often has restrictions/limits as well as permissions/grants to the customer. Often, although not required, this right is perpetual for a particular version of the software package.
- Maintenance: this implies the right to fixes and sometimes support for a particular software package

over a specified period of time. Typically, maintenance is renewed – and the period of time is extended.

- Support: this implies the right to technical help for a particular software package over a specified period of time. Typically, this is renewed so that the period of time is extended.
- Other style: this standard is meant to handle any number of high-level types of entitlement. These may not be fully identified yet – but the standard can be expanded over time.

The content and life cycle for each entitlement type can differ and therefore it is proposed that the following be applied to the standard:

- Entitlement_type is a primitive. It is required for all tags.
- Each entitlement with each unique entitlement type shall have its own tag_id even if it refers to the same product.

As mentioned above, the tag ID should provide an index to the business transaction generating the entitlement and thus SWEID tag.

Inside the SWEID tag

When reading this section, please bear in mind that the ideas expressed are part of a proposed draft of a proposed standard. You may take this as a complete lack of commitment on my part! I can commit, however, to ensuring that my blog at *www.lifecyclestandards.com* contains the latest information, even if only by way of pointers and links to sources of the latest information.

The current ideas on structure

Tag information

Tag_id: as mentioned above, this element contains the unique identifier that can provide an index to the business transaction generating the SWEID tag. It is unique in that it is a complex element type containing a unique ID, which is unique within the domain of the creator, plus the creator's regid.

Parent_id: as mentioned above, this is a linkage to parent tag(s) that originate with the original SWEID tag created. It is unique in that it is a complex element type containing a unique ID, which is unique within the domain of the creator, plus the creator's regid.

Root_id: the tag_ID of the original SWEID as published by the licensor/service provider. It is unique in that it is a complex element type containing a unique ID, which is unique within the domain of the creator, plus the creator's regid.

Tag_type: this shows the type of entitlement as well as its state related to other tags related to this entitlement. A complex element is made up of the tag_type where values might be 'Add', 'Revoke', 'Archive', 'Replacement' or 'Upgrade', and the entitlement_type with possible values of 'Maintenance', 'Renewal', 'True-up' or 'Licence only'.

This element is proposed for use by Symantec Corporation in their tags as follows:

tag_type is an element that indicates the type of SWEID tag – Application, Patch, etc. This field is set to 'Application', 'Patch', 'Group', 'Feature', 'Component'.

Tag_info: this is a complex element containing a mandatory creation date and possibly a modification date.

Tag_creator: this is an exact equivalent form equal to that in the SWID tag above.

Elements_owner: this is a list of elements that is specified as owned by the tag creator. While not as authoritative as a digital signature, it does provide guidance to tag modifiers, implicitly stating that elements contained within the list should not be modified without the express consent of the creator.

Entitlement information

Right: this is a (very!) complex element containing the right type and is really the heart of the entitlement. This element can appear multiple times within a SWEID tag since most entitlements contain multiple rights, including primary, secondary, additional, conditions, etc. Where possible, ISO/IEC standard data definitions are required.

Sub-elements include:

- **Grant**: this is the name of the right, such as install.
- **Quantification**: (mandatory) this is the meter allowed, such as number of seats, terabytes stored or number of cores on platform (yuck!).
- **Time_limit**: (optional) this is the start date and/or end date, tied to GMT. It contains resolution only down to the day level.
- **Geo_limit**: (optional) this is defined down to the country level. It is a list that defines either exclusions or inclusions.

- **Language_limit**: (optional) this defines inclusions or exclusions.
- **Platform_limit**: (optional) this defines inclusions.
- **Environment_limit**: (optional) approved (or not approved) environments for use such as academia, test, disaster recovery, etc.
- **Vm_limit**: (optional) this contains restrictions related to virtual platforms. It indicates if the right is approved for virtual environments plus identification of those environments.
- **Market_limit**: (optional) this is a list of approved or not approved market types.
- **Scope_inclusion**: (optional) this is any term with positive phrasing that does not fit in other limits.
- **Scope_exclusion**: (optional) this is any term with negative phrasing that does not fit in other limits.
- **Condition**: (optional) this is the circumstance for the right to be granted.
- **Additional_attribute**: (optional) this is any term with a neutral phrasing that does not fit into any of the limits.
- **Additional_right**: (optional) this is a secondary right (can cascade through).

Contract_linkage: this is information about the agreement governing the entitlement. This ID may index to a business transaction or contract.

Entitlement_timeframe: this is temporal information about the entire entitlement (rather than just the right as defined above). It contains the same information, such as start date, end date or an indication of a perpetual entitlement.

Entitled_entity: this is a complex element containing information about the end-user of the entitlement, such as name, regid, alias and other additional information.

Previously_entitled: this is used in the case of transfers of entitlement ownership, perhaps due to divestitures, mergers or acquisitions.

Product information

The elements below will reflect what is defined in the SWID equivalent elements listed previously.

Product_title: this is the name of product, as assigned by the software creator. This element has received the support of Symantec Corporation and is used as follows:

Symantec: Used as a display name in reports. Should be normalized with the marketing name for the item that the tag corresponds to. For, example, if the tag is an Application tag, then the product_title should be consistent with how the Application or Product is referenced on entitlement records, marketing/pricing documents, etc. but not include version information. This will allow reports to group based on name across versions. Tools can group based product_title and product_version.name to get a breakdown of titles by version. E.g. Symantec BackupExec, Symantec Endpoint Protection, ...

Product_information: this is additional information about the product the tag relates to, such as:

- Edition – e.g. standard, professional, personal, etc.
- Alias – alternative or more commonly used names for this particular product. For example, some publishers may use the year the product was released or the name of an animal as the common name rather than a one or two-digit number that's incremented with each release.

- Product_family – the product family provides an element that software publishers and software licensors can use to group related software products together for SAM practitioner reports. An example of the type of product that would use this element is a back-up tool where the back-up services, server back-up and client back-up portions for the tool are sold as independent products. In this case, if all products have the same product_family defined, a SAM tool can automatically group discovered software identification tag data appropriately.

Product_version: the element allows software creators to provide purely numeric version information which is used for comparison purposes against software entitlement information and for grouping purposes.

Additionally, the string version is provided so software creators have the ability to specify any textual representation they want an end-user to see in a report.

This element has received the support of Symantec Corporation and is used as follows.

Two sub-elements, name and numeric:

- Name is the string name or marketing name for the version. Example '2010' in the case of BackupExec 2010 or '7.0' in the case of NetBackup 7.0.
- Numeric is the numeric form of the version – major.minor.build.revision. E.g. 9.0.103.1.

Software_creator: this complex element identifies the specific software creator that produced the software package. The element contains name and regid as sub-elements.

Software_licensor: this complex element identifies the specific software licensor that owns the copyright for the software package. The element contains name and regid as sub-elements.

Software_id: the software_id provides information that can be used to reference a specific version of a specific product. This element requires the tag creator to ensure that the unique_id is unique for each software title and version. Different upgrade levels of a software package shall be distinguished by unique software identifiers. To avoid the need for an external registration agency, each tag creator must use their own regid.

The regid is provided along with a unique ID (unique_id) within that regid. Different platforms and/or development environments may have different methods of creating unique IDs. The unique_id could be a GUID or it may be simply a unique reference within the development environment. For example, an organisation could decide that their unique_id would be something like <productname>_<version>_<releaseID>.

It will be possible for multiple tag creators to create their own unique software_ids for the same software product. This is likely to be the case where the software creator did not create a software identification tag (such as for legacy software), and multiple competitive service organisations then create their own tags for use with such software.

This element has received the support of Symantec Corporation and is used as follows.

This is the unique id for the application version and unique for the tag:

- tag_creator_regid – same regid as specified in the software_licensor element.
- unique_id – 'iso-sid-<tag_type>-' + <publisher reference> + '-' + product_title + '-' + product_version.name. <tag_type> ::=

'app' | 'cmp' | 'feature' | 'patch' | 'group'. It should not have any spaces. Use hyphens in place of spaces. Having a standard format will make it easy to visually associate a software_id with the company and the application element it is the tag for. E.g. 'iso-sid-app-symc-BackupExec-2010' which is the Application tag for the BackupExec 2010. 'iso-sid-cmp-symc-BackupExec-Server-2010'.

Other information

Activation: this is a complex element containing information related to the download, installation and activation of the software. This includes:

- registration_code – a value/code provided by the publisher to use when requesting an activation key or serial number
- activation_code – an installation string/code
- download_site – the URL for acquiring ESD and/or registration and/or acquisition of activation codes
- agreement_site – URL of agreement to be acknowledged
- userid – user ID if needed for URLs above
- password – password if needed for URLs above.

Extended_information: this is supplemental information that may be provided by the software or tag creators, the purchaser of the software, or a third party (such as a distributor, SAM tool or desktop management tool).

This element contains any extended information required. Data provided in this section shall be provided in an XML-compliant structure. Additionally, an XSD should be provided so this section can be properly validated. The XSD file shall be referenced properly in the software identification tag XML file as per standard XML definitions.

Sample SWEID tag

Figure 48 shows a SWEID tag I generated with an XSD schema that has close to the final proposed structure.

```
<?xml version="1.0" encoding="utf-8"?>
<tnsa:software_entitlement_tag xmlns:tns="http://www.w3.org/2000/09/xmldsig#"
        xmlns:tnsa="http://localhost/iso/19770/-3/2011/schema.xsd"
        xmlns:xsi="http://www.w3.org/2001/XMLSchema-instance"
        xsi:schemaLocation="http://localhost/iso/19770/-3/2011/schema.xsd
        C:\wamp\www\iso\19770\-3\2011\schema.xsd" id="AAAAA">
 <tnsa:tag_id id="AAAAB">
  <tnsa:tag_creator_regid id="AAAAC">string</tnsa:tag_creator_regid>
  <tnsa:unique_id xsi:type="tnsa:RegistrationId">string</tnsa:unique_id>
 </tnsa:tag_id>
 <tnsa:parent_id id="AAAAD">
  <tnsa:tag_creator_regid>string</tnsa:tag_creator_regid>
  <tnsa:unique_id xsi:type="tnsa:RegistrationId"
id="AAAAE">string</tnsa:unique_id>
 </tnsa:parent_id>
 <tnsa:root_id>
  <tnsa:tag_creator_regid id="AAAAF">string</tnsa:tag_creator_regid>
  <tnsa:unique_id xsi:type="tnsa:RegistrationId"
id="AAAAG">string</tnsa:unique_id>
 </tnsa:root_id>
 <tnsa:tag_type id="AAAAH">
  <tnsa:tag_type id="AAAAI">string</tnsa:tag_type>
  <tnsa:entitlement_type xsi:type="tnsa:RegistrationId"
id="AAAAJ">string</tnsa:entitlement_type>
 </tnsa:tag_type>
 <tnsa:tag_info id="AAABA" />
 <tnsa:tag_creator>
  <tnsa:name xsi:type="tnsa:RegistrationId">string</tnsa:name>
```

```
  <tnsa:regid>string</tnsa:regid>
 </tnsa:tag_creator>
 <tnsa:elements_owner>
  <tnsa:owner_regid>string</tnsa:owner_regid>
  <tnsa:element_id>AAAAA</tnsa:element_id>
 </tnsa:elements_owner>
 <tnsa:elements_owner>
  <tnsa:owner_name xsi:type="tnsa:RegistrationId">string</tnsa:owner_name>
  <tnsa:owner_regid>string</tnsa:owner_regid>
 </tnsa:elements_owner>
 <tnsa:elements_owner id="AAABB">
  <tnsa:owner_regid id="AAABC">string</tnsa:owner_regid>
  <tnsa:element_id>AAAAA</tnsa:element_id>
  <tnsa:element_id>AAAAA</tnsa:element_id>
  <tnsa:element_id id="AAABD">AAAAA</tnsa:element_id>
 </tnsa:elements_owner>
 <tnsa:elements_owner>
  <tnsa:owner_name xsi:type="tnsa:RegistrationId">string</tnsa:owner_name>
  <tnsa:owner_regid>string</tnsa:owner_regid>
  <tnsa:element_id>AAAAA</tnsa:element_id>
 </tnsa:elements_owner>
 <tnsa:elements_owner id="AAABE">
  <tnsa:owner_regid>string</tnsa:owner_regid>
 </tnsa:elements_owner>
 <tnsa:right>
  <tnsa:grant xsi:type="tnsa:RegistrationId">string</tnsa:grant>
  <tnsa:quantification>
   <tnsa:name xsi:type="tnsa:RegistrationId" id="AAABF">string</tnsa:name>
   <tnsa:unit_of_measure>string</tnsa:unit_of_measure>
   <tnsa:quantity id="AAABG">247360051</tnsa:quantity>
```

```
</tnsa:quantification>
<tnsa:time_limit>string</tnsa:time_limit>
<tnsa:language_limit>string</tnsa:language_limit>
<tnsa:environment_limit id="AAABH">string</tnsa:environment_limit>
<tnsa:vm_limit>string</tnsa:vm_limit>
<tnsa:market_limit>string</tnsa:market_limit>
<tnsa:scope_inclusion />
<tnsa:scope_inclusion />
<tnsa:condition />
<tnsa:condition />
<tnsa:additional_attribute />
<tnsa:additional_right>
  <tnsa:grant xsi:type="tnsa:RegistrationId">string</tnsa:grant>
  <tnsa:quantification id="AAABI">
    <tnsa:name>string</tnsa:name>
    <tnsa:unit_of_measure>string</tnsa:unit_of_measure>
    <tnsa:quantity id="AAABJ">2557025959</tnsa:quantity>
  </tnsa:quantification>
</tnsa:additional_right>
<tnsa:additional_right>
  <tnsa:grant>string</tnsa:grant>
  <tnsa:quantification>
    <tnsa:name xsi:type="tnsa:RegistrationId">string</tnsa:name>
    <tnsa:unit_of_measure>string</tnsa:unit_of_measure>
    <tnsa:quantity>1121192622</tnsa:quantity>
  </tnsa:quantification>
</tnsa:additional_right>
<tnsa:additional_right id="AAACA">
  <tnsa:grant id="AAACB">string</tnsa:grant>
  <tnsa:quantification id="AAACC">
```

```
      <tnsa:name id="AAACD">string</tnsa:name>
      <tnsa:unit_of_measure xsi:type="tnsa:RegistrationId"
id="AAACE">string</tnsa:unit_of_measure>
      <tnsa:quantity>215534344</tnsa:quantity>
     </tnsa:quantification>
    </tnsa:additional_right>
   </tnsa:right>
   <tnsa:right>
    <tnsa:grant xsi:type="tnsa:RegistrationId" id="AAACF">string</tnsa:grant>
    <tnsa:quantification>
     <tnsa:name>string</tnsa:name>
     <tnsa:unit_of_measure>string</tnsa:unit_of_measure>
     <tnsa:quantity>3851520512</tnsa:quantity>
    </tnsa:quantification>
    <tnsa:geo_limit>string</tnsa:geo_limit>
    <tnsa:platform_limit id="AAACG">string</tnsa:platform_limit>
    <tnsa:market_limit>string</tnsa:market_limit>
    <tnsa:scope_inclusion />
    <tnsa:scope_inclusion id="AAACH" />
    <tnsa:scope_inclusion id="AAACI" />
    <tnsa:scope_inclusion />
    <tnsa:scope_exclusion />
    <tnsa:scope_exclusion />
    <tnsa:scope_exclusion id="AAACJ" />
    <tnsa:scope_exclusion id="AAADA" />
    <tnsa:condition />
    <tnsa:condition />
    <tnsa:additional_attribute id="AAADB" />
    <tnsa:additional_attribute id="AAADC" />
    <tnsa:additional_attribute id="AAADD" />
    <tnsa:additional_attribute />
```

```
  </tnsa:right>
  <tnsa:right>
    <tnsa:grant id="AAADE">string</tnsa:grant>
    <tnsa:quantification id="AAADF">
      <tnsa:name>string</tnsa:name>
      <tnsa:unit_of_measure
xsi:type="tnsa:RegistrationId">string</tnsa:unit_of_measure>
      <tnsa:quantity>2473999946</tnsa:quantity>
    </tnsa:quantification>
    <tnsa:language_limit id="AAADG">string</tnsa:language_limit>
    <tnsa:environment_limit id="AAADH">string</tnsa:environment_limit>
    <tnsa:vm_limit id="AAADI">string</tnsa:vm_limit>
    <tnsa:market_limit>string</tnsa:market_limit>
    <tnsa:scope_inclusion />
    <tnsa:scope_inclusion id="AAADJ" />
    <tnsa:scope_inclusion id="AAAEA" />
    <tnsa:scope_inclusion id="AAAEB" />
    <tnsa:scope_exclusion />
    <tnsa:scope_exclusion id="AAAEC" />
    <tnsa:condition />
    <tnsa:condition id="AAAED" />
    <tnsa:condition id="AAAEE" />
    <tnsa:condition id="AAAEF" />
    <tnsa:additional_attribute />
    <tnsa:additional_attribute id="AAAEG" />
    <tnsa:additional_attribute />
    <tnsa:additional_attribute id="AAAEH" />
  </tnsa:right>
  <tnsa:right>
    <tnsa:grant>string</tnsa:grant>
    <tnsa:quantification id="AAAEI">
```

```
    <tnsa:name id="AAAEJ">string</tnsa:name>
    <tnsa:unit_of_measure id="AAAFA">string</tnsa:unit_of_measure>
    <tnsa:quantity>3983796914</tnsa:quantity>
  </tnsa:quantification>
  <tnsa:language_limit id="AAAFB">string</tnsa:language_limit>
  <tnsa:platform_limit>string</tnsa:platform_limit>
  <tnsa:market_limit id="AAAFC">string</tnsa:market_limit>
  <tnsa:scope_inclusion id="AAAFD" />
  <tnsa:scope_inclusion id="AAAFE" />
  <tnsa:scope_inclusion id="AAAFF" />
  <tnsa:scope_inclusion id="AAAFG" />
  <tnsa:scope_exclusion />
  <tnsa:condition id="AAAFH" />
  <tnsa:condition id="AAAFI" />
  <tnsa:additional_attribute />
  <tnsa:additional_attribute id="AAAFJ" />
  <tnsa:additional_attribute id="AAAGA" />
  <tnsa:additional_attribute id="AAAGB" />
  <tnsa:additional_right>
    <tnsa:grant xsi:type="tnsa:RegistrationId" id="AAAGC">string</tnsa:grant>
    <tnsa:quantification id="AAAGD">
      <tnsa:name id="AAAGE">string</tnsa:name>
      <tnsa:unit_of_measure id="AAAGF">string</tnsa:unit_of_measure>
      <tnsa:quantity>1601597599</tnsa:quantity>
    </tnsa:quantification>
  </tnsa:additional_right>
</tnsa:right>
<tnsa:right id="AAAGG">
  <tnsa:grant xsi:type="tnsa:RegistrationId">string</tnsa:grant>
  <tnsa:quantification>
```

```
    <tnsa:name xsi:type="tnsa:RegistrationId">string</tnsa:name>
    <tnsa:unit_of_measure xsi:type="tnsa:RegistrationId"
id="AAAGH">string</tnsa:unit_of_measure>
    <tnsa:quantity id="AAAGI">1408461510</tnsa:quantity>
   </tnsa:quantification>
   <tnsa:time_limit>string</tnsa:time_limit>
   <tnsa:platform_limit id="AAAGJ">string</tnsa:platform_limit>
   <tnsa:environment_limit>string</tnsa:environment_limit>
   <tnsa:vm_limit id="AAAHA">string</tnsa:vm_limit>
   <tnsa:market_limit>string</tnsa:market_limit>
   <tnsa:scope_inclusion id="AAAHB" />
   <tnsa:condition id="AAAHC" />
   <tnsa:condition id="AAAHD" />
   <tnsa:condition />
   <tnsa:condition />
   <tnsa:additional_attribute id="AAAHE" />
   <tnsa:additional_attribute id="AAAHF" />
   <tnsa:additional_attribute id="AAAHG" />
   <tnsa:additional_right id="AAAHH">
    <tnsa:grant>string</tnsa:grant>
    <tnsa:quantification>
     <tnsa:name id="AAAHI">string</tnsa:name>
     <tnsa:unit_of_measure>string</tnsa:unit_of_measure>
     <tnsa:quantity id="AAAHJ">1148697593</tnsa:quantity>
    </tnsa:quantification>
   </tnsa:additional_right>
  </tnsa:right>
  <tnsa:contract_linkage id="AAAIA">
   <tnsa:purchase_number xsi:type="tnsa:RegistrationId"
id="AAAIB">string</tnsa:purchase_number>
```

```
  <tnsa:end_user_tracking_number
id="AAAIC">string</tnsa:end_user_tracking_number>
  <tnsa:invoice_no>string</tnsa:invoice_no>
 </tnsa:contract_linkage>
 <tnsa:entitlement_timeframe id="AAAID">
  <tnsa:start_date id="AAAIE">2009-02-12T02:51:50.89</tnsa:start_date>
  <tnsa:end_date>2016-05-07T02:54:11.68</tnsa:end_date>
  <tnsa:is_perpetual>true</tnsa:is_perpetual>
 </tnsa:entitlement_timeframe>
 <tnsa:entitled_entity id="AAAIF">
  <tnsa:name id="AAAIG">2008-09-25T12:32:57.22</tnsa:name>
  <tnsa:regid id="AAAIH">2002-02-27T20:46:13.76</tnsa:regid>
  <tnsa:alias id="AAAII">1</tnsa:alias>
  <tnsa:alias>false</tnsa:alias>
  <tnsa:alias>true</tnsa:alias>
  <tnsa:additional_info id="AAAIJ">0</tnsa:additional_info>
  <tnsa:additional_info>false</tnsa:additional_info>
 </tnsa:entitled_entity>
 <tnsa:previously_entitled id="AAAJA">
  <tnsa:name id="AAAJB">string</tnsa:name>
  <tnsa:regid>string</tnsa:regid>
 </tnsa:previously_entitled>
 <tnsa:product_title>string</tnsa:product_title>
 <tnsa:product_information id="AAAJC">
  <tnsa:product_family xsi:type="tnsa:RegistrationId"
id="AAAJD">string</tnsa:product_family>
  <tnsa:sku>string</tnsa:sku>
 </tnsa:product_information>
 <tnsa:product_version id="AAAJE">
  <tnsa:name xsi:type="tnsa:RegistrationId">string</tnsa:name>
  <tnsa:numeric>
```

```
      <tnsa:major>1015295909</tnsa:major>
      <tnsa:minor>2286236861</tnsa:minor>
      <tnsa:build>143112605</tnsa:build>
      <tnsa:review id="AAAJF">3679464122</tnsa:review>
    </tnsa:numeric>
  </tnsa:product_version>
  <tnsa:software_creator id="AAAJG">
    <tnsa:name id="AAAJH">string</tnsa:name>
    <tnsa:regid id="AAAJI">string</tnsa:regid>
  </tnsa:software_creator>
  <tnsa:software_licensor id="AAAJJ">
    <tnsa:name xsi:type="tnsa:RegistrationId" id="AABAA">string</tnsa:name>
    <tnsa:regid id="AABAB">string</tnsa:regid>
  </tnsa:software_licensor>
  <tnsa:software_id>
    <tnsa:unique_id id="AABAC">string</tnsa:unique_id>
    <tnsa:tag_provider_domain id="AABAD">string</tnsa:tag_provider_domain>
  </tnsa:software_id>
  <tnsa:activation id="AABAE">
    <tnsa:activation_code xsi:type="tnsa:RegistrationId"
id="AABAF">string</tnsa:activation_code>
    <tnsa:password xsi:type="tnsa:RegistrationId">string</tnsa:password>
  </tnsa:activation>
  <tnsa:extended_information>
    <AnyElementYouLike>Some Data Or Other Elements</AnyElementYouLike>
    <AnyElementYouLike>Some Data Or Other Elements</AnyElementYouLike>
    <AnyElementYouLike>Some Data Or Other Elements</AnyElementYouLike>
  </tnsa:extended_information>
  <tnsa:extended_information>
    <AnyElementYouLike>Some Data Or Other Elements</AnyElementYouLike>
  </tnsa:extended_information>
```

```
  <tnsa:extended_information>
    <AnyElementYouLike>Some Data Or Other Elements</AnyElementYouLike>
    <AnyElementYouLike>Some Data Or Other Elements</AnyElementYouLike>
    <AnyElementYouLike>Some Data Or Other Elements</AnyElementYouLike>
  </tnsa:extended_information>
</tnsa:software_entitlement_tag>
```

Figure 48: SWEID test tag

CHAPTER 9: SOFTWARE FEATURE DESIGN RELATED TO SWID/SWEID TAG MANAGEMENT FOR TAG CREATORS AND MODIFIERS

The software life cycle

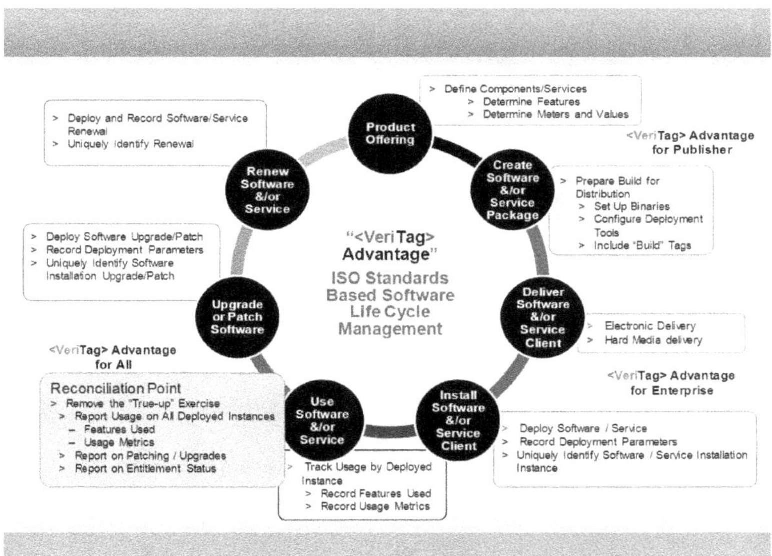

Figure 49: Software/SaaS product life cycle

Figure 49 is a reminder of our life cycle. The first step in the cycle involves the process described in the following sections.

Product tagging and integration life cycle

Figure 50 is an example of the functional sequence that might be followed by a software publisher/OEM that is defining a new product.

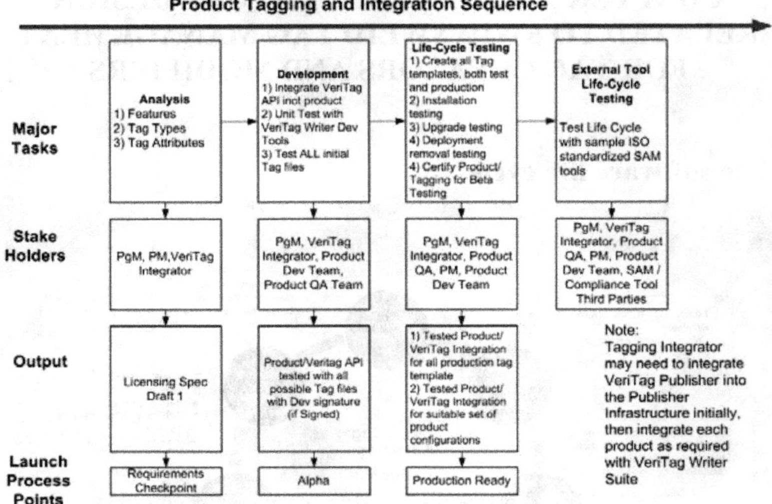

Figure 50: Product tagging and integration sequence

A similar sequence might also be followed if the publisher/OEM has already released a product, but wishes to either:

- simply offer an application patch that updates the installation with SWID tags; or
- include application changes that require patching concurrently with updating the new patched version with SWID tags.

The example sequence shows the use of VTP and VeriTag Writer suite, but the implementer may use any set of SWID tag ISO-compliant management tools to perform the same.

How to analyse your product then design SWEID and SWID tags

The following provides an example of the analysis and design of basic static ISO SWID tags and their associated SWEID tags.

Sample software application – SoftPub Enterprise Firewall (SEF)

SoftPub is a fictitious software publisher that produces firewalls. The product contains many licensable features to which usage entitlement (a licensable for use) is offered and thus may be ultimately deployed and used. Keys are required in order to enable each feature. In order to be able to match entitlement with deployment, a unique SWID tag must be available with the deployed product in order to reconcile the deployment with licensable features.

While there are many licensing models and methods other than the one illustrated here, the approach outlined in this section may be applied to any system of entitlement and deployment.

Licence features and attributes

In the SEF products, a licence comprises several features that enable the various aspects of functionality that are available in the product. Each feature has a set of attributes that further defines the behaviour of the functionality. With the release of SEF 1.0, SoftPub provides a customer with a high degree of flexibility in ordering the SEF product features and attributes that best satisfy the needs of their organisation. Owing to the flexibility offered to the customer, the list of licensable features and their respective attributes is extensive and complex. The next few sections detail these features and attributes.

Features

The base feature for the SEF is the firewall; all other features are add-ons to the base firewall feature. Character strings that are known to both the product and the back-end configuration database represent each of the features within the SWID and SWEID tags. Tables 9 and 10 contain the lists of licensable SEF features and their respective feature strings.

Table 9: SEF base licensable features

SEF function	Licence feature name
Firewall	SEF1.0-FW
S2S	SEF1.0-S2S
Remote VPN	SEF1.0-RVPN
High availability/Load balancing	SEF1.0-HALB
Content filtering	SEF1.0-CF
Content filtering update subscription	SEF1.0-CFS

Table 10: SEF add-on licensable features

Add-on function	Licence feature name
Anti-virus	SEF1.0-AV
Anti-virus definition update subscription	SEF1.0-AVS
Intrusion detection	SEF1.0-IDS
Intrusion detection subscription	SEF1.0-IDSS

SWID tags

The feature for the SEF may be mapped directly on to a SWID tag (and by association, SWEID tag). The name of the tag is prefixed in this example by 'swid' in order to prevent confusion between a licensable feature name and a SWID tag. This is optional, however, and entirely up to the implementer to decide.

Table 11: SEF licensable features and corresponding SWID tag names

SEF function	SWID tag name
Firewall	Swid-SEF1.0-FW
S2S	Swid-SEF1.0-S2S
Remote VPN	Swid-SEF1.0-RVPN
High availability/Load balancing	Swid-SEF1.0-HALB

Content filtering	Swid-SEF1.0-CF
Content filtering update subscription	Swid-SEF1.0-CFS
Add-on function	**SWID tag name**
Anti-virus	Swid-SEF1.0-AV
Anti-virus definition update subscription	Swid-SEF1.0-AVS
Intrusion detection	Swid-SEF1.0-IDS
Intrusion detection subscription	Swid-SEF1.0-IDSS

Licensable feature attributes

Each of the features listed in the previous section has several attributes. All features share many of the attributes, but the details of the attributes often differ. For example, all features have a usage count, but the usage count (meter) available for the SEF1.0-RVPN feature is not the same as the usage count of the other features.

The attributes that are available for the SEF features are:

- Usage count (meter):
  - There are two types of user that are counted as part of the firewall usage count: user licences and server licences. A user licence is counted when the source IP address is from a protected interface (internal). An internal user is allowed to make as many different connections as they like, through many proxies, and this counts as a single user licence. This model is

suitable for situations where internal users are trying to access the Internet. A server licence is counted when the source IP address is not from a protected interface (external).

  - The type of VPN traffic is site-to-site traffic.

- Start date: this is the start date of a licence feature. Content subscription features such as content filtering and anti-virus definition updates always have a start date. All other features may have a start date. Whenever a licensed feature has an end date, it must have a start date as well.
- End date: this is the expiration date of the licensed feature. Content subscription features such as content filtering and anti-virus definition updates always have an expiration date. All other features may have an expiration date.
- Trial: if this is set then the licence is a trial licence and has a start and end date. Trial licences have an unlimited user count.
- Version: the current version of SEF is 1.0.

Table 12: SEF licensable feature attributes

Licence feature name	Feature attributes	SWID tag attributes
SEF1.0-FW	Usage count	25, 50, 100, 250, (unlimited)
	Start date	Start date or <empty>
	End date	Licence expiration date. Typically an empty string –

		unlimited
	Version	1.0
	Trial	1 if trial, 0 otherwise
	Accreditation	<empty> or <organisation>
SEF1.0-S2S	Usage count	(unlimited)
	Start date	Start date or <empty>
	End date	Licence expiration date. Typically an empty string – unlimited
	Version	1.0
	Trial	1 if trial, 0 otherwise
	Accreditation	<empty> or <organisation> (if site licence)
SEF1.0-RVPN	Usage count	5, 25, 100, 250, (unlimited)
	Start date	Start date or <empty>
	End date	Licence expiration date. Typically an empty string – unlimited
	Version	1.0
	Trial	1 if trial, 0 otherwise
	Accreditation	<empty> or <organisation>
SEF1.0-HALB	Usage count	(unlimited)

	Start date	Start date or <empty>
	End date	Licence expiration date. Typically an empty string – unlimited
	Version	1.0
	Trial	1 if trial, 0 otherwise
	Accreditation	<empty> or <organisation>
SEF1.0-CF	Usage count	25, 50, 100, 250, (unlimited)
	Start date	Start date or <empty>
	End date	Licence expiration date. Typically an empty string – unlimited
	Version	1.0
	Trial	1 if trial, 0 otherwise
	Accreditation	<empty> or <organisation>
SEF1.0-CFS	Usage count	25, 50, 100, 250, (unlimited)
	Start date	Start date
	End date	Subscription expiration date
	Hostid	<hostid> or <empty> (if site licence)
	Version	1.0

	Trial	1 if trial, 0 otherwise
	Accreditation	<empty> or <organisation>
SEF1.0-AV	Usage count	25, 50, 100, 250, (unlimited)
	Start date	Start date or <empty>
	End date	Licence expiration date. Typically an empty string – unlimited
	Version	1.0
	Trial	1 if trial, 0 otherwise
	Accreditation	<empty> or <organisation>
SEF1.0-AVS	Usage count	25, 50, 100, 250, (unlimited)
	Start date	Start date
	End date	Subscription expiration date
	Version	1.0
	Trial	1 if trial, 0 otherwise
	Accreditation	<empty> or <organisation> (if site licence)
SEF1.0-IDS		25, 50, 100, 250, SLIC_METERCOUNT_MAX (unlimited)
	Start date	Start date or <empty>

	End date	Licence expiration date. Typically and empty string – unlimited
	Version	1.0
	Trial	1 if trial, 0 otherwise
	Accreditation	<empty> or <organisation>
SEF1.0-IDSS	Usage count	25, 50, 100, 250, SLIC_METERCOUNT_MAX (unlimited)
	Start date	Start date
	End date	Subscription expiration date
	Version	1.0
	Trial	1 if trial, 0 otherwise
	Accreditation	<empty> or <organisation>

Design a SWID tag

Consider the single licensable feature SEF1.0-FW, the base firewall feature.

Table 13: SEF base firewall feature

Licence feature name	Feature attributes	SWID tag attributes
SEF1.0-FW	Usage count	25, 50, 100, 250, (unlimited)

	Start date	Start date or <empty>
	End date	Licence expiration date. Typically an empty string – unlimited
	Version	1.0
	Trial	1 if trial, 0 otherwise

In order to differentiate between the multiple meter values, the publisher may choose to create a separate tag for each meter, i.e. perhaps SEF1.0-FW-25, SEF1.0-FW-50 and so on. Alternatively, these values may be defined in an extended_information tag element as defined by ISO.

Consider the elements of a SWID tag.

Table 14: Elements of a SWID tag

SWID tag attribute	Comment	Proposed value
entitlement_required_indicator	The licensing model description above confirms that a licence key is required. Therefore this can be set to true.	'true'
product_title		'SoftPub Enterprise Firewall V1.0'
product_version	Major, Minor, Build, Review, as selected by the product manager/engineering	'1.0.0.0'

	team.	
software_creator	This can depend upon whether TagVault registration has occurred or not. Assume at this point it has not.	'SoftPub Corporation' and 'www.softpub.com'
Software_licensor	The licence in this case is issued by the creator.	'SoftPub Corporation' and 'www.softpub.com'
software_id	Some ID, unique and generated by SoftPub Corporation.	'fc3cc419-b5a1-9f16-ed203e537c40' and 'www.softpub.com'
tag_creator	Assume here that the corporation is using an ISO-approved copy of VTP and is using this tool to create an ISO-compliant tag internally.	'SoftPub Corporation' and 'www.softpub.com'
Below are some choices for optional attributes. While they may be 'ISO optional' they can be needed in order to understand the correct deployment and licensing model for the product.		
abstract	This is the English language version of the firewall, so the component can also be English (LANG=en).	'This is the base feature for the SEF and is the firewall; all other features are add-ons to the base firewall feature'
complex_of	Since this is the main,	'fc3cc419-b5a1-9f16-

	or base, component of a possible complex of pieces of licensable software, this element is made up of the list of unique identifiers that represent the licensable features or products that make up the complete bundled product. Assume for argument's sake that all features mentioned above are included, a total of 10 components, including the base firewall component.	ed203e537c40' 'fc3cc419-b5a1-9f16-ed203e537c41' 'fc3cc419-b5a1-9f16-ed203e537c42' 'fc3cc419-b5a1-9f16-ed203e537c43' 'fc3cc419-b5a1-9f16-ed203e537c44' 'fc3cc419-b5a1-9f16-ed203e537c45' 'fc3cc419-b5a1-9f16-ed203e537c46' 'fc3cc419-b5a1-9f16-ed203e537c47' 'fc3cc419-b5a1-9f16-ed203e537c48' 'fc3cc419-b5a1-9f16-ed203e537c49'
installation_details	This element can be updated by the automatic installer process (assuming it is installed using a VeriTag Writer-enabled tool). This element is useful for comparison with any licence feature start date, which may be timed with the installation of the product. If the product entitlement is such that the start date coincides	

	with the first time use of the product, the product can need to be enabled for the VeriTag Writer tool so that this element can be updated on first time use.	
product_id	Product_id should be a unique reference, but this can be unique within the software manufacturer and does not need to be a globally unique ID. It is recommended that the Product ID is not the product name or other marketing term as these often change from release to release. Instead, the product_id should be an identifier that can follow products through their life cycle without requiring marketing changes. Product_id is used to define a lineage between products for identification of allowed upgrades.	'fc3cc419-b5a1-9f16-ed203e537c40'
serial_number	Assume here that the corporation is using an ISO-approved copy of VTP which means a tag may be created more than once, but can contain a unique	

	identifier for each creation. This is useful for a publisher that wishes to uniquely identify each SWID, perhaps with each distribution pack generated. In order to achieve this with automation, the VTP must be integrated into the publisher infrastructure so that a tag may be generated automatically as required (on build, on ESD generation, on CD-ROM generation, on entitlement generation, etc.) VTP may be integrated in this fashion. For more information, see the VTP Technical Reference Manual.	
sku	In this particular case, there is a very clear licence linkage with an entitlement that is named, i.e. SEF1.0-FW. Assuming that the publisher maintains mappings of named licence types to SKU(s) (assuming any single licence may be offered through multiple SKUs) in some database, then when reconciliation	'SKU Value'

	occurs, the entitlement type can be reconciled against this element by SKU.	

A tool such as VTP might be used to define the elements within the SWID tag as shown in Figure 51.

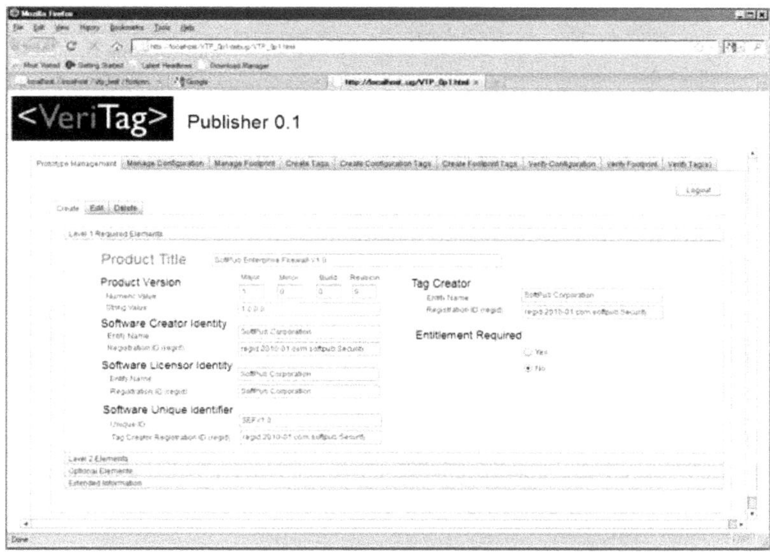

Figure 51: VeriTag Publisher screenshot

This allows input of element data, generation of a SWID tag and subsequent validation of the SWID tag to the level required:

- no certification
- basic certification
- TagVault.org SAM certification.

The resulting SWID tag might look as shown in Figure 52.

```
<?xml version="1.0" encoding="UTF-8"?>

<swid:software_identification_tag id="idvalue0"
xmlns:ds="http://www.w3.org/2000/09/xmldsig#"
xmlns:swid="http://standards.iso.org/iso/19770/-2/2009/schema.xsd"
xmlns:xsi="http://www.w3.org/2001/XMLSchema-instance"
xsi:schemaLocation="http://standards.iso.org/iso/19770/-2/2009/schema.xsd
swid.xsd ">

  <swid:entitlement_required_indicator
id="idvalue1">true</swid:entitlement_required_indicator>

  <swid:product_title id="idvalue2" xsi:type="swid:Token">SoftPub Enterprise
Firewall V1.0</swid:product_title>

  <swid:product_version id="idvalue3">

    <swid:name id="idvalue4" xsi:type="swid:Token">token</swid:name>

    <swid:numeric id="idvalue5">

      <swid:major id="idvalue6">1</swid:major>

      <swid:minor id="idvalue7">0</swid:minor>

      <swid:build id="idvalue8">0</swid:build>

      <swid:review id="idvalue9">0</swid:review>

    </swid:numeric>

  </swid:product_version>

  <swid:software_creator id="idvalue10">

    <swid:name id="idvalue11" xsi:type="swid:Token">SoftPub
Corporation</swid:name>

    <swid:regid id="idvalue12">www.softpub.com</swid:regid>

  </swid:software_creator>

  <swid:software_licensor id="idvalue13">

    <swid:name id="idvalue14" xsi:type="swid:Token">SoftPub
Corporation"</swid:name>

    <swid:regid id="idvalue15">www.softpub.com</swid:regid>

  </swid:software_licensor>

  <swid:software_id id="idvalue16">

    <swid:unique_id id="idvalue17" xsi:type="swid:Token">fc3cc419-b5a1-9f16-
ed203e537c40</swid:unique_id>
```

```
    <swid:tag_creator_regid
id="idvalue18">www.softpub.com</swid:tag_creator_regid>
  </swid:software_id>
  <swid:tag_creator id="idvalue19">
    <swid:name id="idvalue20" xsi:type="swid:Token">SoftPub
Corporation</swid:name>
    <swid:regid id="idvalue21">www.softpub.com</swid:regid>
  </swid:tag_creator>
  <swid:abstract id="idvalue22" lang="en">This is the base feature for the SEF
and is the firewall; all other features are add-ons to the base firewall
feature</swid:abstract>
  <swid:component_of id="idvalue23">
    <swid:software_id id="idvalue24">
      <swid:unique_id id="idvalue25"
xsi:type="swid:Token">token</swid:unique_id>
      <swid:tag_creator_regid id="idvalue26">token</swid:tag_creator_regid>
    </swid:software_id>
  </swid:component_of>
  <swid:complex_of id="idvalue27">
    <swid:software_id id="idvalue28">
      <swid:unique_id id="idvalue29" xsi:type="swid:Token">fc3cc419-b5a1-9f16-
ed203e537c40</swid:unique_id>
      <swid:tag_creator_regid
id="idvalue30">www.softpub.com</swid:tag_creator_regid>
    </swid:software_id>
    <swid:software_id>
            <swid:unique_id>fc3cc419-b5a1-9f16-ed203e537c41</swid:unique_id>
            <swid:tag_creator_regid>www.softpub.com</swid:tag_creator_regid>
    </swid:software_id>
    <swid:software_id>
            <swid:unique_id>fc3cc419-b5a1-9f16-ed203e537c42</swid:unique_id>
            <swid:tag_creator_regid>www.softpub.com</swid:tag_creator_regid>
    </swid:software_id>
```

```
  <swid:software_id>
        <swid:unique_id>fc3cc419-b5a1-9f16-ed203e537c43</swid:unique_id>
        <swid:tag_creator_regid>www.softpub.com</swid:tag_creator_regid>
  </swid:software_id>
  <swid:software_id>
        <swid:unique_id>fc3cc419-b5a1-9f16-ed203e537c44</swid:unique_id>
        <swid:tag_creator_regid>www.softpub.com</swid:tag_creator_regid>
  </swid:software_id>
  <swid:software_id>
        <swid:unique_id>fc3cc419-b5a1-9f16-ed203e537c45</swid:unique_id>
        <swid:tag_creator_regid>www.softpub.com</swid:tag_creator_regid>
  </swid:software_id>
  <swid:software_id>
        <swid:unique_id>fc3cc419-b5a1-9f16-ed203e537c46</swid:unique_id>
        <swid:tag_creator_regid>www.softpub.com</swid:tag_creator_regid>
  </swid:software_id>
  <swid:software_id>
        <swid:unique_id>fc3cc419-b5a1-9f16-ed203e537c47</swid:unique_id>
        <swid:tag_creator_regid>www.softpub.com</swid:tag_creator_regid>
  </swid:software_id>
  <swid:software_id>
        <swid:unique_id>fc3cc419-b5a1-9f16-ed203e537c48</swid:unique_id>
        <swid:tag_creator_regid>www.softpub.com</swid:tag_creator_regid>
  </swid:software_id>
  <swid:software_id>
        <swid:unique_id>fc3cc419-b5a1-9f16-ed203e537c49</swid:unique_id>
        <swid:tag_creator_regid>www.softpub.com</swid:tag_creator_regid>
  </swid:software_id>
</swid:complex_of>
```

```
  <swid:data_source id="idvalue31"
xsi:type="swid:Token">token</swid:data_source>
  <swid:dependency id="idvalue32">
    <swid:software_id id="idvalue33">
      <swid:unique_id id="idvalue34"
xsi:type="swid:Token">token</swid:unique_id>
      <swid:tag_creator_regid id="idvalue35">token</swid:tag_creator_regid>
    </swid:software_id>
  </swid:dependency>
  <swid:elements_owner id="idvalue36">
    <swid:owner_name id="idvalue37"
xsi:type="swid:Token">token</swid:owner_name>
    <swid:owner_regid id="idvalue38">token</swid:owner_regid>
    <swid:element_id id="idvalue39">idvalue0</swid:element_id>
  </swid:elements_owner>
  <swid:installation_details id="idvalue40">
    <swid:location_platform id="idvalue41"
xsi:type="swid:Token">token</swid:location_platform>
    <swid:location_installation id="idvalue42"
xsi:type="swid:Token">token</swid:location_installation>
    <swid:installation_instance id="idvalue43"
xsi:type="swid:Token">token</swid:installation_instance>
    <swid:installation_locale id="idvalue44"
xsi:type="swid:Token">token</swid:installation_locale>
    <swid:installation_target_id id="idvalue45"
xsi:type="swid:Token">token</swid:installation_target_id>
  </swid:installation_details>
  <swid:keywords id="idvalue46">
    <swid:keyword id="idvalue47" xsi:type="swid:Token">token</swid:keyword>
  </swid:keywords>
  <swid:license_linkage id="idvalue48">
    <swid:activation_status id="idvalue49"
xsi:type="swid:Token">token</swid:activation_status>
```

```
    <swid:channel_type id="idvalue50"
xsi:type="swid:Token">token</swid:channel_type>

    <swid:channel_name id="idvalue51"
xsi:type="swid:Token">token</swid:channel_name>

    <swid:customer_type id="idvalue52"
xsi:type="swid:Token">token</swid:customer_type>

  </swid:license_linkage>

  <swid:package_footprint id="idvalue53">

    <swid:external_description
id="idvalue54">http://tempuri.org</swid:external_description>

  </swid:package_footprint>

  <swid:packager id="idvalue55">

    <swid:by id="idvalue56" xsi:type="swid:Token">token</swid:by>

    <swid:part id="idvalue57" xsi:type="swid:Token">token</swid:part>

  </swid:packager>

  <swid:product_category id="idvalue58">

    <swid:UNSPSC_ver id="idvalue59"
xsi:type="swid:Token">token</swid:UNSPSC_ver>

    <swid:segment_title id="idvalue60"
xsi:type="swid:Token">token</swid:segment_title>

    <swid:family_title id="idvalue61"
xsi:type="swid:Token">token</swid:family_title>

    <swid:class_title id="idvalue62"
xsi:type="swid:Token">token</swid:class_title>

    <swid:commodity_title id="idvalue63"
xsi:type="swid:Token">token</swid:commodity_title>

    <swid:code id="idvalue64">0</swid:code>

  </swid:product_category>

  <swid:product_family id="idvalue65"
xsi:type="swid:Token">token</swid:product_family>

  <swid:product_id id="idvalue66" xsi:type="swid:Token">fc3cc419-b5a1-9f16-
ed203e537c40</swid:product_id>

  <swid:release_date id="idvalue67">2001-12-31T12:00:00</swid:release_date>

  <swid:release_id id="idvalue68" xsi:type="swid:Token">token</swid:release_id>
```

```
<swid:release_package id="idvalue69">
  <swid:sign_off id="idvalue70" xsi:type="swid:Token">token</swid:sign_off>
  <swid:sign_off_date id="idvalue71">2001-12-
31T12:00:00</swid:sign_off_date>
  <swid:by id="idvalue72" xsi:type="swid:Token">token</swid:by>
</swid:release_package>
<swid:release_rollout id="idvalue73">
  <swid:sign_off id="idvalue74" xsi:type="swid:Token">token</swid:sign_off>
  <swid:sign_off_date id="idvalue75">2001-12-
31T12:00:00</swid:sign_off_date>
  <swid:by id="idvalue76" xsi:type="swid:Token">token</swid:by>
</swid:release_rollout>
<swid:release_verification id="idvalue77">
  <swid:sign_off id="idvalue78" xsi:type="swid:Token">token</swid:sign_off>
  <swid:sign_off_date id="idvalue79">2001-12-
31T12:00:00</swid:sign_off_date>
  <swid:by id="idvalue80" xsi:type="swid:Token">token</swid:by>
</swid:release_verification>
<swid:serial_number id="idvalue81"
xsi:type="swid:Token">E12345678</swid:serial_number>
<swid:sku id="idvalue82" xsi:type="swid:Token">SEF-1P0-EDU-25</swid:sku>
<swid:software_creator_alias id="idvalue83">
  <swid:alias id="idvalue84">
    <swid:alias_name id="idvalue85"
xsi:type="swid:Token">token</swid:alias_name>
    <swid:alias_regid id="idvalue86">token</swid:alias_regid>
  </swid:alias>
</swid:software_creator_alias>
<swid:software_licensor_alias id="idvalue87">
  <swid:alias id="idvalue88">
    <swid:alias_name id="idvalue89"
xsi:type="swid:Token">token</swid:alias_name>
```

```
      <swid:alias_regid id="idvalue90">token</swid:alias_regid>
    </swid:alias>
  </swid:software_licensor_alias>
  <swid:supported_languages id="idvalue91">
    <swid:language id="idvalue92" xsi:type="swid:Token">token</swid:language>
  </swid:supported_languages>
  <swid:tag_creator_alias id="idvalue93">
    <swid:alias id="idvalue94">
      <swid:alias_name id="idvalue95"
xsi:type="swid:Token">token</swid:alias_name>
      <swid:alias_regid id="idvalue96">token</swid:alias_regid>
    </swid:alias>
  </swid:tag_creator_alias>
  <swid:tag_creator_copyright id="idvalue97"
lang="en">swid:tag_creator_copyright</swid:tag_creator_copyright>
  <swid:tag_version id="idvalue98">
    <swid:name id="idvalue99" xsi:type="swid:Token">token</swid:name>
    <swid:regid id="idvalue100">token</swid:regid>
    <swid:numeric_version id="idvalue101">
      <swid:major id="idvalue102">0</swid:major>
      <swid:minor id="idvalue103">0</swid:minor>
      <swid:build id="idvalue104">0</swid:build>
      <swid:review id="idvalue105">0</swid:review>
    </swid:numeric_version>
  </swid:tag_version>
  <swid:upgrade_for id="idvalue106">
    <swid:upgrade_id id="idvalue107">
      <swid:unique_id id="idvalue108"
xsi:type="swid:Token">token</swid:unique_id>
      <swid:tag_creator_regid id="idvalue109">token</swid:tag_creator_regid>
    </swid:upgrade_id>
```

```
<swid:upgrade_description id="idvalue110"
xsi:type="swid:String">swid:upgrade_description</swid:upgrade_description>
</swid:upgrade_for>
<swid:usage_identifier id="idvalue111">
<swid:filename id="idvalue112" xsi:type="swid:Token">token</swid:filename>
<swid:processname id="idvalue113" type="literal">token</swid:processname>
<swid:URI id="idvalue114" type="literal">token</swid:URI>
</swid:usage_identifier>
<swid:validation id="idvalue115">
<swid:validation_call id="idvalue116"
xsi:type="swid:Token">token</swid:validation_call>
<swid:last_validated_by id="idvalue117"
xsi:type="swid:Token">token</swid:last_validated_by>
<swid:last_validated_date id="idvalue118">2001-12-
31T12:00:00</swid:last_validated_date>
<swid:last_validated_result id="idvalue119"
xsi:type="swid:Token">token</swid:last_validated_result>
</swid:validation>
<ds:Signature Id="idvalue120">
<ds:SignedInfo Id="idvalue121">
<ds:CanonicalizationMethod Algorithm="http://tempuri.org"/>
<ds:SignatureMethod Algorithm="http://tempuri.org">
<ds:HMACOutputLength>0</ds:HMACOutputLength>
</ds:SignatureMethod>
<ds:Reference Id="idvalue122" Type="http://tempuri.org"
URI="http://tempuri.org">
<ds:Transforms>
<ds:Transform Algorithm="http://tempuri.org">
<ds:XPath>ds:XPath</ds:XPath>
</ds:Transform>
</ds:Transforms>
<ds:DigestMethod Algorithm="http://tempuri.org"/>
```

```
      <ds:DigestValue>0</ds:DigestValue>
    </ds:Reference>
  </ds:SignedInfo>
  <ds:SignatureValue Id="idvalue123">0</ds:SignatureValue>
  <ds:KeyInfo Id="idvalue124">
    <ds:KeyName>ds:KeyName</ds:KeyName>
  </ds:KeyInfo>
  <ds:Object Encoding="http://tempuri.org" Id="idvalue125" MimeType="">
    <ds:SPKIData>
      <ds:SPKISexp>0</ds:SPKISexp>
    </ds:SPKIData>
  </ds:Object>
 </ds:Signature>
 <swid:extended_information id="idvalue126"/>
</swid:software_identification_tag>
```

Figure 52: SWID base tag

The resulting SWID tag should be verified with TagVault.org as compliant and entered in the TagVault.org tag registry.

How to use the tags

Step two in our life cycle, the 'Create Software &/or Service Package' step in Figure 4, involves injecting the initial SWID tags, sometimes referred to as build tags, into the build or 'bag of bits'.

These SWID tags then become available for insertion into the consumer infrastructure at install/deployment time, the 'Install Software &/or Service Client' step in Figure 4.

The third step in the cycle, the 'Deliver Software &/or Service Client' step in Figure 4, requires that automation be added to the delivery infrastructure, either as a custom step or via acquisition from the many companies now engaging in ISO/IEC 19770 technology.

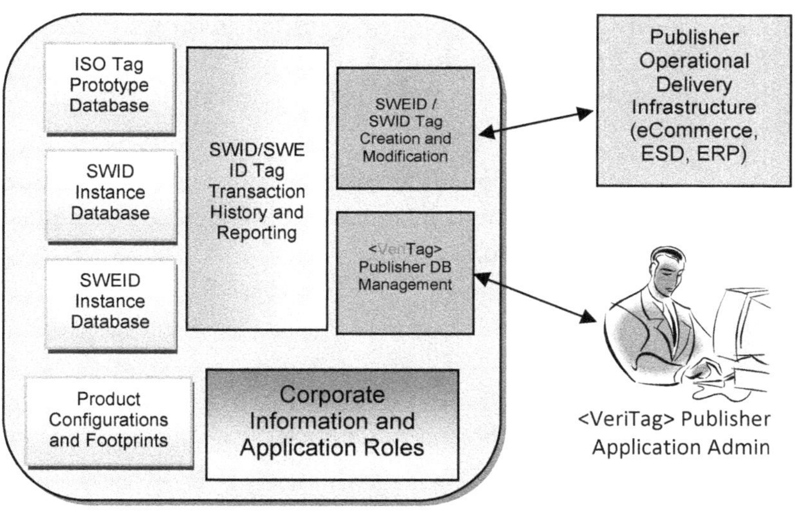

Figure 53: VeriTag Publisher architecture

Figure 53 shows a very high-level architectural view of what this means.

The fulfilment/delivery infrastructure may be interfaced to deliver both SWID and SWEID tags.

The SWEID tag

SWEID tags are created and delivered as a result of some business transaction performed possibly by the ERP (sales of a licensed SKU) or perhaps a customised buying programme infrastructure that issues entitlements according to some contract.

Each SWEID tag may be uniquely identified (using the paradigms described earlier) and indexed back to the transaction within the publisher's infrastructure. In order to assist the consumer, perhaps a reference number provided by the consumer during the business transaction might be included in the SWEID tag.

At this point, both consumer and creator have a standard record of the entitlement instance, which can be referenced in either infrastructure.

The SWID tag

The SWID tag(s) will be delivered as part of the distribution 'bag of bits'. Conceivably the tag will be the build tag only; however, it is possible that the build tag might form a prototype for a uniquely identifiable SWID tag that is indexed to the generation or delivery (especially in the case of ESD) of the distribution. This delivery may in itself be indexed back to the business transaction, allowing at least partial matching of subsequent deployments of the distribution to the business transaction.

Allowing measurement of usage with SWID tags

There is a paradigm of SWID tagging whereby the SWID tag is extended, using the ISO/IEC 19770-2:2009 definition, to capture true usage information. The technique works with both SaaS client and licensed software, and requires active participation of the installed software.

Symantec will be introducing this type of functionality with their products in the near future. Measurement of usage will include basic activity plus metrics and feature use over time.

CHAPTER 10: SWID AND SWEID TAG MANAGEMENT FOR CONSUMERS

The software life cycle

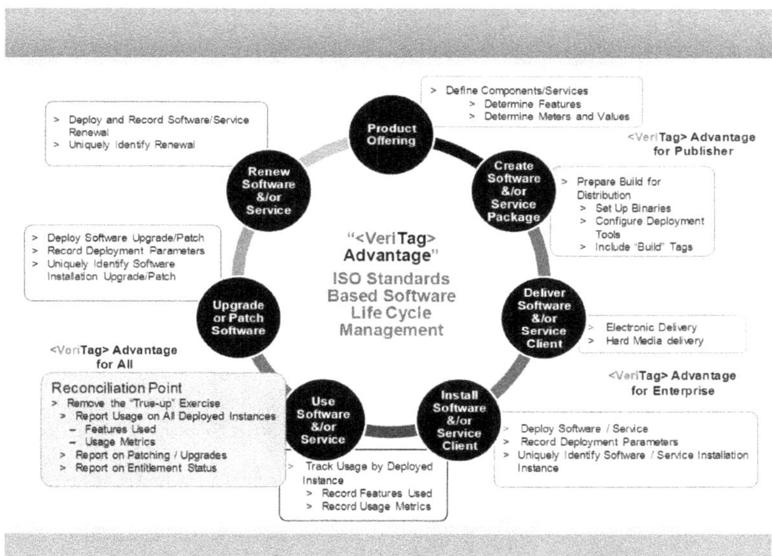

Figure 54: Software/Saas product life cycle

Figure 54 is a reminder of our life cycle. The third step in the cycle involves both the publisher/creator as well as the consumer. The publisher delivers both SWID and SWEID tags; the consumer receives them.

The SWEID tag

The SWEID tag may be recorded directly into some form of entitlement database, an example of which is shown in Figure 55.

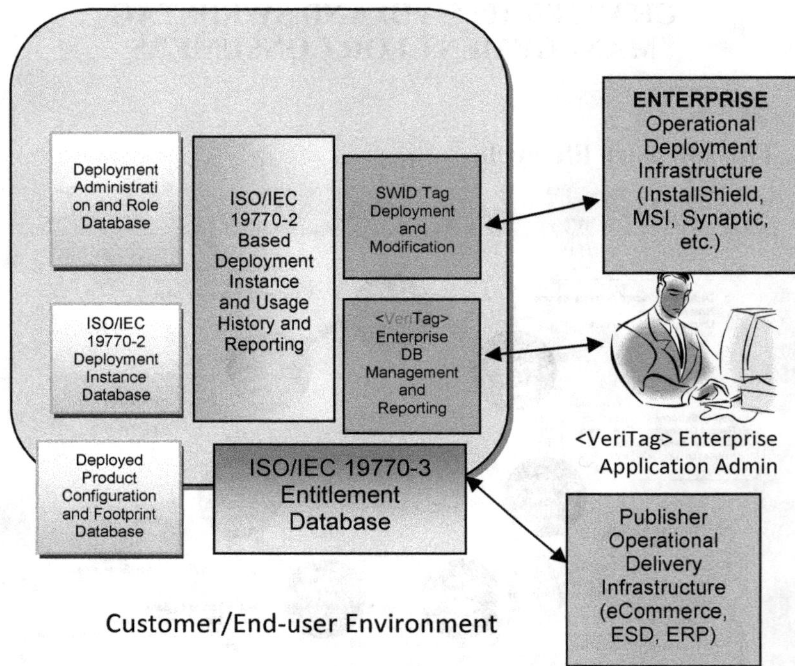

Figure 55: VeriTag Enterprise architecture

The task requires that:

- the publisher issues SWEID tags as per the standard and delivers them in a manner in which the consumer may accept them
- the consumer has the process and supporting infrastructure to process SWEID delivery.

The SWID tag

SWID tags of the build variety may arrive as part of a publisher distribution and if so, as part of the 'Install Software &/or Service Client' step in Figure 54, will be deployed automatically on each computing device that the software is installed upon using the standard installer as supplied by that same publisher.

Subsequent software deployment and usage management information may be derived by using SAM tools that are compliant with the ISO/IEC 19770-2:2009 standard to harvest and report on this information.

Altiris, a Symantec business unit, will be releasing this functionality with their management tools in the near future.

Another option is to either modify the installation tools to record the deployment information in a configuration management database (CMDB) that supports the SWID data format, or even to go to the next level and execute the installation inside standard processes using tools, examples of which are currently available and widely used, to populate a CMDB automatically.

Following this process allows each deployment to be installed with a uniquely identifiable SWID tag(s) and include deployment information, using the ISO/IEC 19770-2:2009 elements described earlier on, allowing for very precise management information being available further on in the life cycle.

Usage, upgrades and renewals

Without implementation of SWEID tags, there is currently not much leverage to be gained in managing renewals unless a publisher of SaaS clients adopts the usage paradigm mentioned in the previous chapter, thus allowing client-side usage management. It remains to be seen how this notion is adopted going forward.

Similarly the usage reporting of licensed software, with the exception of that currently planned by Symantec, is restricted to whether a software product is deployed and/or possibly running.

Upgrade and patching information may be tracked in the same fashion as initial installs.

The reconciliation point

I have already discussed the 'two hands clapping' metaphor earlier. Until the SWEID is accepted by ISO and fully adopted by publishers and service providers, the case is very much 'one hand clapping'. If you are a student of Zen, this should be a familiar koan and thus can only be related to your own context.

If, however, you have or can acquire a record of your entitlement purchases, the task of reconciliation can be made easier with the use of SWID tag information, describing deployments and usage at their most primitive level.

Currently, even SWID tags are not being issued as a matter of process by publishers. Notable exceptions to this are Symantec and Adobe.

SKU element considerations within the SWID tag

In its simplest form, the process of reconciliation is required for each licence feature, eventually to be manifested by a SWEID tag, and an associated SWID tag.

Any given licensable function may be sold in many ways. For example, using the example shown earlier, licensable function SEF1.0-FW-25 may be sold as shown in Table 15.

Table 15: SEF base SKU

SKU description	SKU	Comment
SEF 1.0 1420 25 NODE BASE GOV	SEF-1P0-GOV-25	The SKU for the licensable feature as sold to government
SEF 1.0 1420 25 NODE BASE EDU	SEF-1P0-EDU-25	The SKU for the licensable feature as sold to education (as in the example SWID tag in Figure 52)
SEF 1.0 1420 25 NODE BASE USA	SEF-1P0-USA-25	The SKU for the licensable feature as sold to USA region enterprise
SEF 1.0 1420 25 NODE BASE EMEA	SEF-1P0-EMEA-25	The SKU for the licensable feature as sold to Europe, Middle East and Africa region enterprise

If the SKU element in the SWID tag is not correctly formatted in the distribution for each of these SKU types, reconciliation becomes more difficult, since reconciling with the correct entitlement becomes less precise.

In order to achieve this, it is important that the SWID tag generator is integrated appropriately with the publisher infrastructure (as described earlier) in order to facilitate this process. VeriTag Publisher is designed to interface in this fashion from the outset.

Frankly, it is not clear that there is a clear business argument in my own mind that can justify a publisher attempting to uniquely identify SWID tags other than to attempt to increase customer satisfaction. However, as an idealist, I live in hope.

More likely is the scenario presented earlier of identifying each SWID tag from the installation process, which of course may or may not relate to the entitlement SKU associated with the deployment.

Overcoming the inertia of ISO/IEC 19770 adoption by software publishers

Oh, the pain that is involved for both those proposing and those adopting any new standard! Of course, how can a standard be truly considered a standard unless it is commonly used (or used at all!). If this particular paradigm did not seem to solve so many problems in my opinion, I would be condemning it to the endless abyss of thoughts and ideas where many a creative notion has come to rest.

What may appear to be a major roadblock to the consumer – the adoption of the tagging standards by publishers and service providers – may not be an insurmountable hurdle.

There is the concept of SWID tag retrofitting, elements for which exist within the ISO/IEC 19770-2:2009 definition. That is to say, it is possible to add SWID tags to existing software deployments, as well as maintain the infrastructure by adding SWID tags to upgrades, changes and new software as they enter the infrastructure.

Of course, an immediate question would be... Why?

After some considerable research and calculation, I have derived the following.

SWID tag retrofitting, saving on reconciliation expense

I used some figures for the true-up exercise that seem to be typical of use as a measuring stick by most. If you are someone who has to manage this exercise on a day-to-day basis, you will already have a good idea, and actually I would like feedback on your experience if possible.

I used the following sample configuration:

- 50 servers
- 1,500 workstations.

Estimated cost of a manual biannual true-up

Time taken

- Full software true-up of 1,550-machine organisation – 100+ working days (~US$100K).

True-up costs

- True-up of 500 workstations – $150.00/machine per event
- True-up for Adobe of 250 instances – ~$75.00/machine per event

- True-up for Oracle of 30 instances – ~$450/machine per event
- True-up for IBM of 50 server instances – ~$350/machine per event.

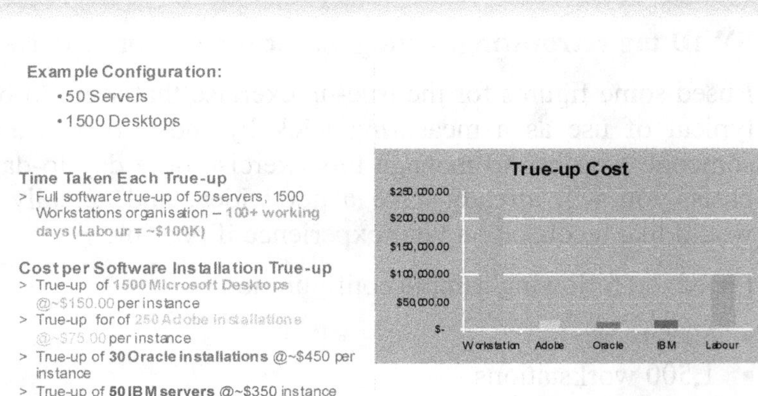

Manual True-up Event
Example Configuration:
• 50 Servers
• 1500 Desktops
Time Taken Each True-up
> Full software true-up of 50 servers, 1500 Workstations organisation – 100+ working days (Labour = ~$100K)
Cost per Software Installation True-up
> True-up of 1500 Microsoft Desktops @~$150.00 per instance
> True-up for of 250 Adobe installations @~$75.00 per instance
> True-up of 30 Oracle installations @~$450 per instance
> True-up of 50 IBM servers @~$350 instance
True-up Cost
$250,000.00
$200,000.00
$150,000.00
$100,000.00
$50,000.00
$-
Workstation
Adobe
Oracle
IBM
Labour
Total Cost = $375,000 PER TRUE-UP EVENT
every year? every 2 years ?...

Figure 56: Manual biannual true-up

Estimated cost of a SWID tagging-assisted annual true-up

The calculation below assumes a cost of ~$10 per SWID tag deployed as an overhead on SWID tagging.

Time taken

- Full software true-up of 1,550-machine organisation – 15–20 working days.

Cost – six-year total ~$2.4M

Annual tag-assisted true-up of $25K, which assumes every product upgrades annually and thus requires each and every tag updated and redeployed:

- Tags for 1,500 workstations – $30.00/machine/install or upgrade
- Tags for Adobe 250 machines – ~$30.00/machine/install or upgrade
- Tags for Oracle of 30 instances – ~$80/machine/install or upgrade
- Tags for IBM of 50 server instances – ~$100/machine/install or upgrade.

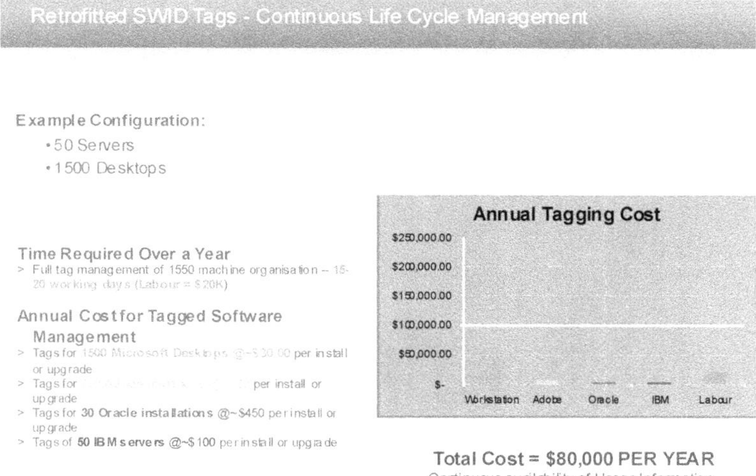

Figure 57: Software management with SWID tagging true-up

Challenges to the process

The first annual event requires a full manual true-up in order to establish the install data upon which to build. Thus there is a considerable overhead in this first year, which is illustrated in Figure 58.

Working on the premise that the publisher has not designed or produced SWID tags (unless your only suppliers are Symantec or Adobe!) for the software components found, this task must be performed. The process is described in the previous chapter.

There are now services becoming available from consulting and SAM practitioners that will perform this service as part of a true-up exercise.

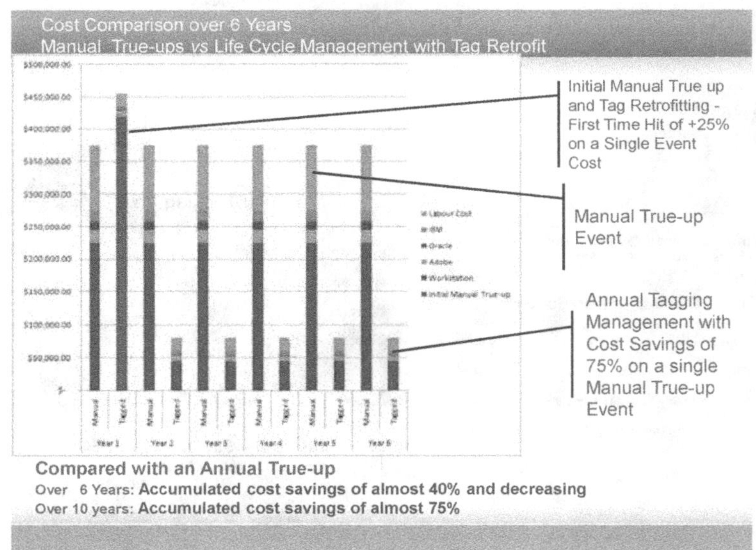

Figure 58: Cost comparison over six years

The resulting SWID tags are verified and registered with TagVault.org as a step in the process and as a result the number of TagVault-compliant SWID tags is constantly increasing. The SWID tags that already exist may reflect deployments found in multiple consumer infrastructures. By default, TagVault.org allows these SWID tags to be used by members of the organisation.

Advantages to the process

For each year after the initial true-up year, it is assumed that every product receives at least one patch or upgrade per year, thus a complete set of SWID tags is required each year at a further $10.00/tag. Additional manual effort is required for the true-up in assembling reports, etc.

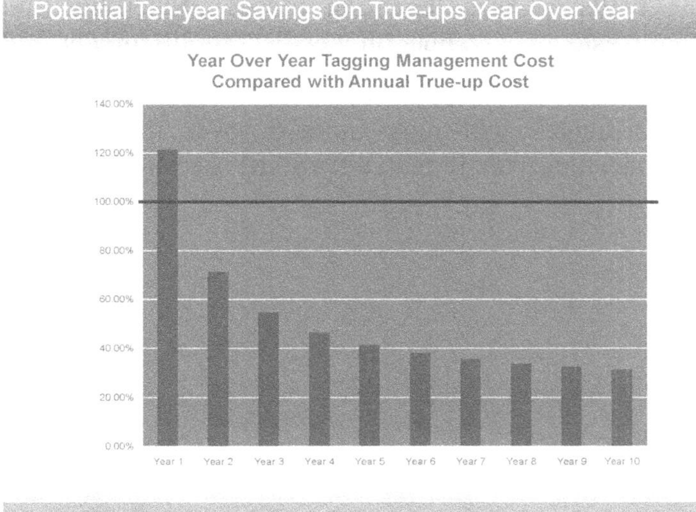

Figure 59: Potential savings year over year for 10 years

I am predicting a reduction in cost, a higher frequency of true-ups occurring, plus, if the CMDB is available, up-to-date deployment management reporting will be available any time.

As can be seen in Figure 59, the longer-term potential savings can be considerable, even if the figures shown are considered optimistic. The economic advantages are clear, even if my estimates on true-up vary by 50%.

Conclusion

I hope I have shown that economic advantages for the enterprise software consumer exist from even the current state of the ISO/IEC 19770-2:2009 standard as well as the upcoming ISO/IEC 19770-3 standard in that IT resources may be better utilised, enabling more productivity and reducing waste of revenue on needless entitlements and supporting infrastructure costs.

These advantages will only increase over time as the standard becomes exactly that, a standard used by most.

APPENDIX: ISO/IEC 19770-2:2009 XML SCHEMA DEFINITION (XSD)

The following XSD provides the definition for the software tag. This XSD file is located at the following location: *http://standards.iso.org/iso/19770/-2/2009/schema.xsd*.

Owing to copyright considerations regarding ISO plus the ease of public access, which is encouraged by ISO, I have not reproduced the listing here.

GLOSSARY

Configuration management database (CMDB) – database containing all the relevant details of each configuration item and details of the important relationships between them.

Configuration item (CI) item – aggregation of hardware or software or both that is designed to be managed as a single entity.

Note 1: CIs may vary widely in complexity, size and type, ranging from an entire system including all hardware, software and documentation, to a single module or a minor hardware component.

Note 2: this document refers primarily to software CIs.

Entitlement – installation or execution rights for a software CI, valid for a predefined time period and based upon software licence purchases.

Extensible mark-up language (XML) – licence-free and platform-independent mark-up language that carries rules for generating text formats that contain structured data.

Globally unique identifier (GUID) – pseudo-random, 16-byte string of characters that is generated in a manner that gives a very high probability that the string is unique in any context.

Identity element – component of a software tag describing a common attribute of most or all software CIs.

Line-of-business application developer – person or company specialising in developing applications providing specific functions that are important to the success of a particular business function.

Licence – contract between a software manufacturer and a customer stipulating terms, conditions and rights of usage.

Platform – computer or hardware device and/or associated operating system.

Release – collection of new and/or changed CIs which are tested and introduced into a production environment together.

Release manager – individual responsible for implementing release management processes, primarily those relating to software development, packaging and distribution.

Software asset – an entitlement or licence for use of any software resource, whether it be a software program, service or some form of content used in association with a software resource.

Software asset management (SAM) – effective management, control and protection of software assets within an end-user organisation.

SAM owner – individual at a senior organisation-wide level who is identified as being responsible for SAM.

SAM practitioner – individual involved in the practice or role of working with software assets. Typically, a SAM practitioner is involved in the collection or reconciliation of software inventory and/or entitlements.

Software life cycle management – the end-to-end management, regardless of role (publisher, OEM, consumer), of all associated software assets for a software product.

Software manufacturer – person, group or company that develops software.

Software provider – any organisation or person that is creating software for use on computing devices. These may include software manufacturers or line-of-business application developers.

Software publisher – person, group or company that packages and distributes software. The publisher may or may not be a software manufacturer as well.

Software entitlement identification (SWEID) tag – file comprising identity elements containing authoritative identification information about a software entitlement.

Software identification (SWID) tag – file comprising identity elements containing authoritative identification information about a software CI.

Value-added reseller (VAR) – company licensed to repackage and support existing products as combined software packages.

ITG RESOURCES

IT Governance Ltd. sources, creates and delivers products and services to meet the real-world, evolving IT governance needs of today's organisations, directors, managers and practitioners.

The ITG website (*www.itgovernance.co.uk*) is the international one-stop-shop for corporate and IT governance information, advice, guidance, books, tools, training and consultancy.

Other Websites

Books and tools published by IT Governance Publishing (ITGP) are available from all business booksellers and are also immediately available from the following websites:

www.itgovernance.co.uk/catalog/355 provides information and online purchasing facilities for every currently available book published by ITGP.

www.itgovernance.eu is our euro-denominated website which ships from Benelux and has a growing range of books in European languages other than English.

www.itgovernanceusa.com is a US$-based website that delivers the full range of IT Governance products to North America, and ships from within the continental US.

www.itgovernanceasia.com provides a selected range of ITGP products specifically for customers in South Asia.

www.27001.com is the IT Governance Ltd. website that deals specifically with information security management, and ships from within the continental US.

Pocket Guides

For full details of the entire range of pocket guides, simply follow the links at *www.itgovernance.co.uk/publishing.aspx*.

Toolkits

ITG's unique range of toolkits includes the IT Governance Framework Toolkit, which contains all the tools and guidance that you will need in order to develop and implement an appropriate IT governance framework for your organisation. Full details can be found at *www.itgovernance.co.uk/products/519*.

For a free paper on how to use the proprietary Calder-Moir IT Governance Framework, and for a free trial version of the toolkit, see *www.itgovernance.co.uk/calder_moir.aspx*.

There is also a wide range of toolkits to simplify implementation of management systems, such as an ISO/IEC 27001 ISMS or a BS25999 BCMS, and these can all be viewed and purchased online at: *http://www.itgovernance.co.uk/catalog/1*.

Best Practice Reports

ITG's range of Best Practice Reports is now at *www.itgovernance.co.uk/best-practice-reports.aspx*. These offer you essential, pertinent, expertly researched information on a number of key issues including Web 2.0 and Green IT.

Training and Consultancy

IT Governance also offers training and consultancy services across the entire spectrum of disciplines in the information governance arena. Details of training courses can be accessed at *www.itgovernance.co.uk/training.aspx* and descriptions of our consultancy services can be found at *http://www.itgovernance.co.uk/consulting.aspx*. Why not contact us to see how we could help you and your organisation?

Newsletter

IT governance is one of the hottest topics in business today, not least because it is also the fastest moving, so what better way to keep up than by subscribing to ITG's free monthly newsletter *Sentinel*? It provides monthly updates and resources across the whole spectrum of IT governance subject matter, including risk management, information security, ITIL and IT service management, project governance, compliance and so much more. Subscribe for your free copy at: *www.itgovernance.co.uk/newsletter.aspx*.

EU for product safety is Stephen Evans, The Mill Enterprise Hub, Stagreenan, Drogheda, Co. Louth, A92 CD3D, Ireland. (servicecentre@itgovernance.eu)

www.ingramcontent.com/pod-product-compliance
Lightning Source LLC
Chambersburg PA
CBHW061219220326
41599CB00025B/4689

* 9 7 8 1 8 4 9 2 8 2 0 4 8 *